D1194760

John Morley

WALPOLE

Elibron Classics
www.elibron.com

Edition de Luxe

THE WORKS

OF

LORD MORLEY

IN

FIFTEEN VOLUMES

VOLUME XIII

WALPOLE

BY

JOHN VISCOUNT MORLEY
O.M.

MACMILLAN AND CO., LIMITED
ST. MARTIN'S STREET, LONDON
1921

CONTENTS

CHAPTER I

CHAPTER II

CHAPTER III

CHAPTER IV

CHAPTER V

CHAPTER VI

CHAPTER VII

CHAPTER VIII

CHAPTER IX

CHAPTER X

CHAPTER XI

CHAPTER I

WALPOLE was born in August 1676. He came fifth among nineteen children born to Mr. Robert Walpole, a country gentleman of Norfolk, of good estate and ancient lineage. The founder of the family had come over with William of Normandy, and the stock had shown its vigour by an unbroken descent in the male line for no fewer than eighteen generations. Walpoles had been knights of the shire as far back as Edward II. Edward Walpole, grandfather of the future minister, sat in the Convention Parliament of 1660. He is said to have acquired a respectable character for eloquence and weight ; he voted for the restoration of Charles II., and he was made a Knight of the Bath. Robert, his son, was in Parliament from the Revolution until his death in 1700. An active Whig in politics, he was a man of marked prudence and credit in his private conduct. A good name in those days was not incompatible with a jovial temper and much steady drinking. Mr. Walpole was fond of sport, fond of farming and business, and fond of plenty of company and plenty of Nottingham ale. He always took care of his money. An old book, in which he set down all his expenses, showed that he knew how to live in London for upwards of three months for the moderate sum of sixty-five pounds seven shillings and fivepence. Mr. Walpole sent his third son to Eton and to King's College at Cambridge, not because he valued education, even if education could now have been obtained in those famous foundations, but because he designed the young man to push his fortunes in the Church, then the usual field for a cadet of decent family. But the youth had higher destinies before him than fat livings and an easy bishopric. His elder brother died in 1698, and Robert the younger, becoming heir to the family estates, quitted the university, and settled down with his convivial father to learn all that pertains to the management of land and the enjoyment of country life. It is said that Robert the elder used to insist on making his son drink more than his just share, on the ground that no son should ever be allowed to have enough of his senses to see that his father was tipsy. Amid such surroundings, which, though compared with the more polished surface of modern manners they seem coarse and rough, yet were vigorous, hearty, and practical, Walpole reached his twenty-fourth year. His father vowed that he would make him the first grazier in the country. Higher destinies were in store for him. The young squire, under a homely exterior, covered a powerful understanding, a strong will, a good eye for men, and a union of solid judgment with commanding ambition, which fitted him to rule a kingdom, and to take his place among the foremost men in Europe.

In the summer of 1700 he married Miss Catherine Shorter, grand-daughter of Sir John Shorter, once Lord Mayor of London. The lady brought him beauty, good manners, and a fortune. Before the end of the year his father died at the early age of fifty, and Robert Walpole came into the estate. Nearly the whole of it lay in the county of Norfolk, and as it was then let, the rent-roll amounted to something over two thousand pounds a year. The property carried with it a couple of pocket boroughs, Castle Rising and Lynn. Mr. Walpole was at once (January 1701) elected for the first of them, rendered vacant by his father's decease, and he retained the seat until the death of King William. In 1702, on the accession of Queen Anne, he was returned for Lynn Regis ; he continued to sit for the same borough without interruption until his fall from power forty years later. It is sometimes said that the advance of democracy has destroyed this stability of relation between representatives and constituents ; but it is worth noting that two members of the existing House of Commons (1889) have held what are virtually the same seats without a break, one of them for fifty-nine years, and the other for fifty-four.

The moment of Walpole's entrance upon parliamentary life was one of critical importance in national history. The great question which had been opened and provisionally closed by the events of 1688, was whether the English monarchy should be limited and Protestant, or absolute, Catholic, and dependent on France. The work of the Revolution may seem at this distance of time to have been out of danger by the beginning of the eighteenth century. Even if it were true that the bulk of the nation had made up its mind, this is not always a guarantee against surprise and against accident, as an incident of a later generation may serve to show. France in 1873 had made up its mind for a Republic, yet only a personal caprice, or stubborn principle, in the Comte de Chambord saved France from a legitimist restoration. The calamity of a legitimist restoration in England was only avoided by the sagacity and the resolution, first of the king, and then of the Whig leaders.

Walpole joined the Whigs in supporting the

Act of Settlement, but he is not known to have taken part in debate. Personal emulation is stated to have been the spur that first made him a speaker. At Eton he had been the schoolfellow, if not the rival, of a lad who was destined to one of the most singular careers in political history. St. John, better known by his later title of Bolingbroke, was two years younger than Walpole, and he entered Parliament about the same time. He had not been many months in the House of Commons before gifts of incomparable brilliancy brought him to the very front place among the debaters of his time. The occasion of Walpole's maiden speech is not known. All that is told is that he was confused and embarrassed, and failed to realise the expectations of his friends. He was followed by somebody more fluent than himself. " You may applaud the one," said an acute onlooker, " and ridicule the other, as much as you please ; but depend upon it, the spruce gentleman who made the set speech will never improve, and Walpole will in time become an excellent speaker." Walpole took pains to fulfil the prediction by relying on his native qualities ; he was active in business, attentive to all that went on, keen in observing men and watching opportunity, and staunch to the principles and the party that he had adopted for his own.

Walpole was first introduced into government —that important moment in the life of a member of Parliament—in a subordinate post on the council of Prince George of Denmark. The appointment was made on the recommendation of no less important a personage than Marlborough. The prince was the queen's husband, and because he was the husband of the queen, he had been made Lord High Admiral of England. The naval board had provoked bitter complaints of mismanagement, negligence, and corruption, and the leading Whigs, not yet fully reconciled with the administration of Marlborough and Godolphin, whose transformation was still incomplete, actively echoed the outcry of the merchants against the Lord High Admiral and his advisers. Walpole said the best that could be said for his colleagues, and when he was reproached with the terrible sin of speaking against some of his own party, he answered with spirit that he would never be so mean as to sit at a board and not defend it. At the same time, as he had to defend the board, he did his best to improve it. In this inferior office he first showed those qualities of a great man of business which, along with his extraordinary general power of mind and character, afterwards made him a great minister. Godolphin, then the head of the government, was himself a man of business just short of the very first class. The contemporary authorities tell us that Walpole won his chief's admiration by his energy and punctuality in affairs, his precision in accounts, his insight into finance, and his easy manners. In a short time he was called upon to exhibit these qualifications in a more important field.

The first Parliament of Anne was strongly Tory. The House of Lords, numbering before the Union with Scotland about one hundred and ninety members, including the bishops and the Catholic peers who could not sit, contained the representatives of the great families who had made and guided the Revolution of 1688. Here, therefore, the Whigs held a uniform predominance. But they had no share in the leading posts of administration for three years after the accession of the queen. Marlborough and Godolphin were the two heads of Anne's first government, and they remained so until the great ministerial revolution in 1710. During this period of eight years the government passed through no fewer than three important changes. First Marlborough and Godolphin were

joined by the high Tories, with the Earl of Nottingham at their head. Then in 1704 the high Tories
were displaced, and Godolphin took in the more
moderate and, we must add, the more unprincipled
section of the same party, in the persons of Harley
and St. John. They were brought in as the
particular friends of Marlborough, and were meant
by him to balance the Whig influence of Cowper
and Sunderland. It was to be not government
by parties, but government by groups. Finally,
the General and the Treasurer, as the two leaders
were called, found themselves slowly driven to
look in the Whig direction, and in 1706 they
pressed the Earl of Sunderland into the government, against the vehement wishes of the queen,
and to the great displeasure of their colleagues.
Halifax told them they were mixing oil with
vinegar. The uneasy combination lasted until
the beginning of 1708. It then fell to pieces, and
government by groups came necessarily to an end.
Harley's furtive ambitions, spurred on by the restless and intrepid St. John, made any subordinate
position privately irksome to him. He began,
in Bishop Burnet's phrase, to set up for himself,
and to act no more under the direction of the
Lord Treasurer. Where anything was to be got,
said his bitterest enemy in later years, Harley
always knew how to wriggle himself in ; when
any misfortune threatened, he knew how to wriggle
himself out. A bedchamber revolution helped him.
The Treasurer and the General soon discovered
Harley's practices ; they went to the queen, and
finding her unwilling to part with him, declared
themselves bound to quit her service. The scene
that followed is a curious example of the difference in ministerial procedure between that time
and our own. The day was Sunday, and a
Cabinet Council had already been summoned. The
queen in those days sat at their meetings, just

as she systematically attended on all important discussions in the House of Lords, and was even upon one occasion personally appealed to by Marlborough in the course of the debate in that chamber. After Marlborough and Godolphin had left the presence, Anne immediately went to the Cabinet Council. "Harley," says Burnet, "opened some matters relating to foreign affairs: the whole board was very uneasy; the Duke of Somerset said he did not see how they could deliberate on such matters, since the General was not with them; he repeated this with some vehemence, while all the rest looked so cold and sullen that the Cabinet Council was soon at an end; and the queen saw that the rest of her ministers and chief officers were resolved to withdraw from her service if she did not recall the two that had left it." It was said, the writer goes on to tell us, that she was ready to put all to the hazard, but the caution and timidity of Harley prevented her. She sent for Marlborough the next day, and after some expostulations told him that Harley would go. Anne's resentment was deep, and though she was obliged to take the two leaders back into her service, they never recovered either her favour or her confidence. The important fact during the first eight years of the reign of Queen Anne is not that the administration was first Tory, then composite of Whig and Tory, and in its final stage pure Whig, but that it was in all its stages, whether Whig or Tory, a Marlborough administration, seconding the policy, providing means for the projects, and devoted to the person of that great and powerful genius.

This was the most important of the three changes that preceded the great party revolution of the last four years of the reign. It brought about that government by a particular political connection which Burke some sixty years later

singled out as the grand illustration, furnished by
one of the most fortunate periods in our history,
of the virtue of Party. " These wise men," he
said, " for such I must call Lord Sunderland,
Lord Godolphin, Lord Somers, and Lord Marlborough, were too well principled in those maxims
upon which the whole fabric of public strength
is built, to be blown off their ground by the breath
of every childish talker. They were not afraid
that they should be called an ambitious junto ;
or that their resolution to stand or fall together
should, by placemen, be interpreted into a scuffle
for places." Godolphin now for the first time
formed his government on a basis exclusively
Whig. It was on this occasion, in the spring of
1708, that Walpole was made Secretary for War
in the room of St. John.

The Lord Treasurer was far from being a mere
figurehead. Godolphin was one of the men of a
type that a great revolution seldom fails to throw
up—silent, able, pliant, assiduous, indispensable.
He was the younger son of a Cornish gentleman.
The Godolphins made their first appearance in
public life in the latter half of the sixteenth century,
and the fortunes and influence of their house grew
so rapidly that throughout the seventeenth century
their only rivals in Cornwall were the Grenvilles.[1]
It was to the head of the house of Godolphin, as
his most honoured friend, that Hobbes dedicated
the *Leviathan*. His brother, Sidney, is described
by Clarendon as a young gentleman of incomparable
parts, who being of delicate education and constitution, and unacquainted with contentions, upon
his observation in the House of Commons of the
wickedness of the king's enemies, out of the pure
indignation of his soul and conscience to his country,

---

[1] See p. 45 of W. Prideaux Courtney's *Parliamentary Representation
of Cornwall to 1832*—an excellent piece of work, of especial interest in
connection with Walpole, who owed so much to Cornish boroughs.

engaged himself with the royalists. The Sidney Godolphin of Queen Anne was of less delicate mould. He began his career as a page in the household of Charles II., and at the same time, oddly enough, he had, like Harley, entered the House of Commons as member for one of the twenty - two parliamentary constituencies which Cornwall at that time possessed. From 1626 to 1766 a Godolphin had been returned thirty-seven times for Helston, and with a very brief interruption the minister held the seat until his elevation to the peerage. Charles used to say of him, that Sidney Godolphin was never in the way and never out of the way. He guarded the public Treasury with the jealous watchfulness of a miser over his hoard. He resisted a job, even when it was backed by the mighty influence of Marlborough, and when he sanctioned a warrant for the supply of a new silver trumpet for a troop of the Guards, he minuted it with an inquiry what had become of the old one. All governments were equally indifferent to him, and he took care not to make himself impossible either at Kensington or at St. Germains. Before the death of Charles II. Godolphin had risen to be a peer and First Commissioner of the Treasury. James II. made him chamberlain to the queen, and he was often bitterly reproached in after years for the exuberant complacency with which he had attended his royal mistress to her papistical devotions. After William of Orange had landed, and James was about to leave Whitehall, Godolphin was one of the five Lords whom he left to represent him in his absence. This did not prevent him from immediately acquiring in turn the confidence of King William, or from resuming his post at the Treasury, the one Tory in a Whig administration. Then for a while he withdrew, but before long he was again First Commissioner, and while he was thus the trusted servant of William, he secretly took

pains to send messages to James at St. Germains
that no kindness from the usurper could ever make
him forget his duty to his lawful king. This was
the shiftiness of the times. It did not prevent
Pope from praising Patritio's hand unstained, his
uncorrupted heart, his comprehensive head (*Moral
Essays*, i. 80). By a strange paradox, the most
solid and precise financier of his day was one of
the most inveterate gamesters : " His pride was
in piquet, Newmarket fame, and judgment at a
bet." It delivered him, he said, from the necessity
of talking. Godolphin was at least free from the
vice of personal rapacity. His probity at the
Exchequer was absolutely unstained. When he
died, after more than five - and - twenty years of
nearly continuous public employment, he left no
larger sum behind him than twelve thousand
pounds. It has been justly contended on his
behalf that a financier who could year after year
raise the vast sums that were required for Marlborough's great campaigns without public disturbance, and without serious detriment to the national
credit, must have been a minister of extraordinary
skill, capacity, and resource.

Besides this strong testimony to his ability,
Godolphin's ministry will always be remembered
in connection with one domestic event of the highest
degree of political importance : I mean the in-
corporating union between England and Scotland.
This was a transaction that abounded in delicate
issues. Many sober judges despaired of ever seeing the consummation of so momentous a treaty.
Those who were most sanguine expected the
negotiations to be protracted for several years.
With an expedition that was of happy omen, the
matter was begun and closed within the compass of a single year. Brilliant as was the lustre,
and real as was the importance of Blenheim
and Ramillies, Oudenarde and Malplaquet, those

glorious days were infinitely less fruitful in fortunate consequences to the realm than the 6th day of March 1707, when Queen Anne went down to the House of Lords and gave the royal assent to the Act approving and ratifying the Treaty of Union between the two kingdoms henceforth to be known as Great Britain.

The immediate consequences of the measure were not favourable to the ministers who carried it. The Union involved the admission of Presbyterians to Parliament, and this strengthened the cry, which was so loud during the first fifteen years of the century, that the Church was in danger. The exclusion of Harley, St. John, and the Tories from government had sent the Church over into violent opposition. The disappearance of the measure against Occasional Conformity heightened the alarm, and an Act (1709) for nationalising all foreign Protestants who had settled in England, was full of offence to the inflamed partisans of a national Establishment. At the general election of 1705 the clergy and the universities had spread over the country tragic apprehensions of the danger of the Church, but Marlborough's victories were an irresistible argument on the other side. In the general election three years later,—for the reader will not forget that this was the time of triennial Parliaments,—the drum ecclesiastic had again been beaten, with no better result to the High Churchmen in Parliament. A reaction was near at hand, and prudent observers like Walpole may well have foreseen it.

The tide was undoubtedly setting against the Whigs. But in politics the occasion is everything. The general current of the time may be for a government or against a government, yet the breaking of the wave often depends upon some small incidental thing done or left undone. Godolphin gratuitously furnished his antagonists with the occasion that was wanted, and the great crisis came rapidly to a head in a wholly unexpected form. In disturbed times an important feature is the calendar of political fasts and festivals. The commemoration of anniversaries has always marked dangerous moments in the recent history of French government, and on a humbler scale in the annals of Ireland since the Union. The political saints'-days in England in the reign of Anne were the 30th January, the date of the martyrdom of the blessed King Charles I.; the 29th May, the birthday and the day of the restoration of his blessed son, King Charles II.; and the 5th November, the day on which, in 1605, the king and the three estates of the realm had their wonderful escape from the most traitorous and bloodily-intended massacre by gunpowder,—and the day on which also, by a striking coincidence, William of Orange had landed at Torbay eighty-three years later for the deliverance of our Church and nation. Sermons on these famous dates then, and for many years to come, gave an opportunity too good to be lost for talking violent politics. A sermon at St. Paul's was like a modern demonstration in Hyde Park, and the great controversy between Hoadley, of St. Peter-le-Poer, and Blackhall, of St. Mary Aldermary, excited the same kind of interest as Newport programmes and Midlothian manifestoes. Dr. Price's discourse at the dissenting meeting-house in the Old Jewry on 4th November 1789 laid the train for Burke's *Reflections on the French Revolution.* It was Dr. Sacheverell's sermon on 5th November 1709 that provoked the most violent Tory explosion of the century. Sacheverell was a clergyman of respectable family, a Fellow of Magdalen College, Oxford, and preacher of St. Saviour's Church, Southwark. He possessed no marked ability, but he had some of the gifts of the pulpit, and was a popular city preacher on the Tory side. Addison had been his contemporary and friend at Magdalen, and is supposed to have dedicated one of his early poems to him. In a sermon in 1702 he had boasted that he hung out "a bloody flag and banner of defiance" against all dissenters, and the pleasant phrase gave lively satisfaction to his friends. His historic discourse at St. Paul's on 5th November 1709 is vehement, heated, and uncompromising, and it contains much strong language about dissenters, and the false brethren who connived at dissent; but it hardly deserves to be dismissed as absurd and scurrilous. It was a bold declaration, without qualification or exception, of the general principle of passive obedience and non-resistance to government, with practical innuendoes that pointed unmistakably against the whole Revolution settlement. The Lord Mayor, who was among the congregation at St. Paul's and who was a Tory member of Parliament, thanked the preacher for his sermon, took him home to dinner, urged him to publish it, and accepted the dedication. Forty thousand copies found buyers.

The government felt that this was an attack on the existing order that could not be passed over. Marlborough, Somers, and Walpole inclined to the view that it might be left to an ordinary prosecution at law. Godolphin, however, stung by a nickname cast upon him by Sacheverell, supported the violent and impetuous Sunderland in urging impeachment; and this course was resolved upon. As events turned out, the decision was disastrous to the government and to the Whig party. The error was not wholly without excuse. The great constitutional battle was not yet secure, and if Sacheverell's sermon meant anything, it meant condemnation of the principles of the Revolution, of the settlement of the Crown, and of the Act and the policy of Toleration.

Historians, looking merely to the result, are for the most part of opinion that the impeachment was impolitic and a blunder. Burke on the contrary, in whose political circle all the circumstances of the fall of the Whigs in 1710 must have remained as a living tradition, seems to approve of the impeachment. It seldom happens to a party, he says in a familiar passage of the *Appeal from the New to the Old Whigs*, to have the opportunity of a clear, authentic, recorded declaration of their political tenets upon the subject of a great constitutional event. The Whigs made that opportunity. " The impeachment of Dr. Sacheverell was undertaken by a Whig ministry and a Whig House of Commons, and carried on before a prevalent and steady majority of Whig peers. It was carried on for the express purpose of stating the true grounds and principles of the Revolution. It was carried on for the purpose of condensing the principles on which the Revolution was first opposed and afterwards calumniated, in order by a juridical sentence of the highest authority to confirm and fix Whig principles, as they had operated both in the resistance to King James, and in the subsequent settlement, and to fix them in the extent and with the limitations with which it was meant that they should be understood by posterity."

Walpole was appointed to be one of the managers for the impeachment, and, though he had not favoured the step in council, he was its most energetic agent in the House of Commons. His arguments and those of his colleagues on one side, taken along with those of Sir Simon Harcourt and Bishop Atterbury on the other side (if Atterbury was the author of the Doctor's speech in his own defence), are a complete and satisfactory presentation of the two party positions.

The commotion itself has been so often described

that it is unnecessary to tell over again here how
Sacheverell became the hero of the hour; how
each day during the three weeks of his trial he was
attended by an immense crowd of zealous admirers
rending the air with their huzzas, and struggling
to kiss his hand as he went from his lodging in the
Temple along the Strand to Westminster Hall;
how his effigies were sold in every street; how his
health was drunk before the queen's and in the
same glass with that of the Church; how the
London mob attacked meeting-houses, burned the
pews and furniture, and maltreated all who would
not shout as they did; and how they pressed
round the queen herself in her sedan-chair at the
door of Westminster Hall, crying, " God bless
your Majesty and the Church, we hope your
Majesty is for Dr. Sacheverell." He was as
popular in the provinces as in the capital; his
journey through the midlands to a living in Shrop-
shire was like a royal progress; and the book-
sellers sold more copies of his trial than of anything since Dryden's *Absalom and Achitophel*. The
final sentence was lenient enough to satisfy even
the half-contemptuous indulgence of modern days.
When the trial was over, the Lords decreed that
he should be suspended from preaching for three
years, and that his sermon should be publicly
burnt, along with some other obnoxious matters
and things, in the presence of the Lord Mayor
and the Sheriffs of London.

Walpole published a pamphlet in the shape of
four letters on this whole transaction, when all
was over; proving " in clear and familiar language,
and by a plain but strong deduction of reasoning,
that the abettors of Sacheverell were the abettors
of the Pretender; and that those who agreed
with him to condemn such resistance as dethroned
the father, could have no other meaning than
the restoration of the son." What was much more

important was the practical moral that was drawn by Walpole for his own use. It gave him an aversion and horror at any interposition in the affairs of the Church, and led him to assume occasionally a line of conduct towards Nonconformists which appeared even to militate against those principles of general toleration to which he was naturally and by creed inclined.

CHAPTER II

EMBOLDENED by this extraordinary manifestation
of sentiments with which she was privately in
such strong sympathy, the queen proceeded to
change her ministers with as much eagerness as
George III. showed in dismissing Mr. Fox on the
defeat of his India Bill in 1783. Her new advisers
did not at once dare to displace Marlborough from
his command, but with that important exception the
administration was substantially changed. Harley,
at first taking only the office of Chancellor of the
Exchequer, was the mainspring of the new government, and was shortly installed as Lord Treasurer.
Harcourt was first Lord Keeper and then Lord
Chancellor, and Rochester was made President of
the Council. The most important of all the appointments was that of St. John as Secretary of
State. It is interesting to note that this is the
last occasion on which a prelate of the Church
was made a member of a government. The Bishop
of Bristol became Lord Privy Seal.

The general election of 1710 was conducted
with extraordinary violence, especially in the large
towns. Boisterous crowds barred the way to the
polling booth, and in many places there was open,
flagrant, and brutal intimidation. The clergy
placed themselves at the head of the agitation.
They filled their sermons with inflammatory
topics ; they went about from house to house

pressing their flocks to show on this great occasion
their zeal for the Church ; they assured them that
now or never was the time to deliver their queen
from the bondage in which her late ministers had
kept her. The result was a great victory for the
new men. When people tell us that our present
popular franchise is responsible for what are styled
the violent turnover majorities of recent political
history, it is well to remember that fluctuations at
least as remarkable took place on the old system in
the exciting and critical decade at the beginning of
the eighteenth century. There has never been a more
rapid electoral transition than that from the great
Whig majority in 1708, to the great Tory majority
in 1710. Two hundred and seventy members lost
their seats. The installation of the Tory ministry
was the first strong attempt to break the Whig
chain, the first vigorous effort in the long struggle
between the Crown and that party, which did not
finally close until the victory of the younger Pitt
over Fox in 1784. Ranke has justly observed
that Queen Anne's last administration is what
gives her reign its marked character in English
history.

One of the first measures in the new Parliament
was a vindictive attack, according to the fierce
spirit of the time, upon the fallen ministers. Serious
efforts had been made by Harley to induce Walpole
to remain. It was not in Harley's designs to
make a clean sweep, and the history of the Godolphin administration is enough to show that a clean
sweep was not yet the accepted principle of a
change of government. The sovereign was still
free to man each department of state as she thought
fit, without paying more attention than she pleased
to the wishes of her chief adviser, or to the relations
of a given minister with his colleagues. The collective feeling and principle which is the foundation of the modern Cabinet did not then exist.

Harley from the outset looked for Whig aid to protect him against the highfliers among his own allies. He gave it out that "a Whig game was intended at bottom," and made earnest advances to Walpole, telling him that he was as good as half of his party put together. Walpole was too long-headed to accept the flattering invitation. His strong and straightforward mind had already grasped the cardinal truth that it was no longer possible for a mixed and composite government to deal with the immense difficulties of the time, and that only a vigorous, concentrated, and continuous administration could be trusted to bring the country through its dangers. He refused Harley's solicitations, though, by a singular variation from modern official usage, he retained for several months after the Whig ministry had been broken up the place of Treasurer of the Navy, which he had held along with the office of Secretary for War.

When the majority had opened their great attack on Godolphin's management of the public purse, to the effect that the enormous sum of thirty-five millions sterling was unaccounted for, Walpole published a couple of replies, effectually disposing of the charge against his chief, and securing for himself the character of the best man of figures of his time. He was so successful that his adversaries declared it to be the one thing needful to get him out of the House. The charge against him was that he had corruptly received a thousand pounds in connection with a contract for forage while he was Secretary for War. It was resolved (January 1712) that Mr. Walpole had been guilty of a high breach of trust and notorious corruption, that he should be committed to the Tower, and that he should be expelled from the House and disqualified for re-election during the Parliament. Notwithstanding this resolution the borough of Lynn at once proceeded again to elect him, and he was again expelled, thus furnishing the closest precedent to the more famous constitutional case of Wilkes and the electors of Middlesex sixty years afterwards. Walpole published a strenuous vindication of himself while he lay in the Tower, but it is not satisfactory according to the salutary rigour of modern standards of administrative purity. He had undoubtedly not received a shilling for himself out of the contract, but he had bargained that his friend should receive a share in it, and the contractors had bought out the friend by payment of a thousand pounds. We should all be horrified at such good nature at the public expense in any modern minister, but the fact that Walpole made no personal gain completely exonerated him with his contemporaries.

Upon his release at the close of the session, Walpole was much too keen a party man, and too honestly interested in the great national issues at stake, to be an idle onlooker. He wrote various political pieces, and he magnanimously and cheerfully performed that indefinable and mystic function which is so highly valued by the parliamentary whipper - in, and known as keeping the party together. The hospitality with which he entertained his political associates, we are told, endeared him to the party and animated their counsels. A story is told, that he paid a farewell visit to Godolphin, who lay dying at one of the houses of the Duchess of Marlborough at St. Albans (1712); and that the old statesman, pointing to Walpole, urged her never to forsake him, "for if souls are permitted to return to the earth, I will appear to reproach you for your conduct."

The great achievement of the Tory administration was the Peace of Utrecht (1713). "I am afraid," says Bolingbroke with cynical frankness, "that

we came to court in the same dispositions as all
parties have done ; that the principal spring of
our actions was to have the government of the
state in our hands ; that our principal views were
the conservation of this power, great employments
to ourselves, and great opportunities of rewarding
those who had helped to raise us, and of hurting
those who stood in opposition to us." At the same
time he held that the Peace, though the only solid
foundation for a Tory system, was also a necessity
and a blessing both for the country and for Europe.
No transaction in our annals has ever given rise to
more violent and protracted disputes. It is one
of the landmarks of European history, like the
treaties of Münster in the seventeenth century,
of Paris and of Versailles in the eighteenth, and of
Vienna in the nineteenth. It effected an astonishing aggrandisement of the position of England in
Europe, it made wider room for her polity and her
trade in the New World, and it inflicted sufficient
humiliation on her two most powerful rivals in
the Old. For twelve years England, the Empire,
and Holland had carried on war against the House
of Bourbon in France and in Spain. Marlborough,
as the General-in-Chief of the allies, in face of the
extraordinary difficulties inseparable from the management of a confederacy so great, so complex,
with such diverse interests, had won year after
year a series of mighty victories over the French,
which can only be compared to the crushing defeats
inflicted on the European monarchies a hundred
years later by Napoleon Bonaparte. At the
moment when Queen Anne dismissed Godolphin,
the great English general had Louis XIV. at his
mercy. With the fall of the Whigs all was changed.
France once more raised her head. The allies
heard the news from London with profound dismay.
The Dutch exchanged their ordinary phlegm for
anger and consternation. But Bolingbroke and

Harley did not shrink. The victorious soldier, whose career for so many years had been an unbroken tale of triumph in marches, sieges, battles, and negotiations, was dismissed from his commands, as if he were the worst of public offenders, instead of being the deliverer of Europe and the glory of his country. The deposition of Marlborough was as truly one chief aim in pushing the Peace of Utrecht, as one chief aim in the Peace of Paris fifty years later was the deposition of Pitt. In days of a settled dynasty like our own, it is hard to realise the apprehensions inspired by Marlborough's ascendancy. But in 1710 Oliver Cromwell had been dead little more than fifty years. Men were nearer to the Protectorate than we are to the great Reform Bill. All the circumstances of the Protectorate were living facts in the memory of the nation. There was nothing incredible or unimaginable in the notion of a great soldier seizing the authority of the State. Marlborough had acquired immense wealth ; the Emperor had wished to make him Governor of the Austrian Netherlands ; he was a Prince of the Empire ; he had, in an unwise moment, pressed the queen to make him Captain-General for life. So extraordinary a career was thoroughly calculated to exalt his imagination and inflame his ambition. It was true that he would have no successor in the male line, and this, among other things, made the shrewder Tories doubtful about the existence of the boundless designs that were freely imputed to him by the bulk of their party. Such dark suspicions as these, however, were not needed to establish the advantage of pulling down the man who was the chief tower of Whig strength.

The Opposition were quite as keenly alive to the party aspects of the Peace as were the government. They assailed the Treaties, Walpole among the foremost, with a vehemence that has never been

surpassed. We were breaking, they said, our most
solemn engagements with the allies. We were
betraying the Dutch. We were still leaving the
crowns of France and Spain on the heads of two
princes of the House of Bourbon. We had covered
ourselves with dishonour ; we had flung away the
fruits of twelve years of struggle and of victory ;
and we had wantonly, shamefully, and wickedly
rejected the opportunity of once for all delivering
Protestant England and Protestant Holland from
the pretensions at once of the Most Christian and
of the Most Catholic king.

Nobody can dispute that the Whigs had that
supreme object of parliamentary desire, a strong
debating case. The English government, in con-
cealing from their allies the negotiations which
they were secretly carrying on with the common
enemy, acted with a degree of fraud and duplicity
that was worthy of ancient Greece or mediaeval
Italy. Even Frederick the Great never did anything so base as the statesmen who sent their
general to Holland with express instructions actually to checkmate their own ally on the very field
of battle. Bolingbroke's methods must be stamped
by every impartial historian with indelible infamy.
The betrayal and abandonment of the Catalans
was truly criminal. But on the merits, and viewed
in the light of subsequent events, the Peace must
be pronounced to have been the true policy. It is
ridiculous to attribute to Bolingbroke or his party
the fruits of the Peace. The fruits were gathered
at Utrecht, but they had been secured by twelve
years of war. The sacrifices of England were in
some degree repaid by the extension of her possessions. She retained from Spain the famous rock
of Gibraltar, Port Mahon and the Isle of Minorca.
France surrendered Nova Scotia, Newfoundland,
and Hudson's Bay. The fortifications of Dunkirk
were to be dismantled. By a provision which

to-day is regarded with horror, England was to
be allowed to supply the Spanish possessions
in America with negro slaves. More respectable
clauses were those which extorted from the bigoted
king the release of subjects who had been cast into
prison for their religion, and a definite recognition
of the Protestant line in Great Britain, as well
as the expulsion of the Pretender from French
territory. Against these substantial gains were
undoubtedly to be set the risks of some counter-
balancing mischiefs. But the mischiefs never came
to pass, and the way was made ready for that long
period of European tranquillity with which the
name of Walpole is for ever so honourably bound
up.

Harley was the first of the four statesmen who,
within the next hundred years, ascended from the
Speaker's chair to be heads of government.[1] When
the Tory administration was formed, the Treasury
was put in commission, but not many months
later Harley, as has already been stated, was made
Lord High Treasurer ; he left the House of Commons, became the Earl of Oxford and Mortimer,
and finally received the distinction of the Garter.

The ministers had come in upon the flood tide
of a great reaction. Experience has often shown
the dangers of these triumphant situations. The
new men speedily found themselves in difficulties.
The queen's design had been to break up the Whig
junto, to break up government by party, and by
ending the war to destroy the towering ascendancy
of Marlborough. Harley, during three years of
back-stairs intrigue, had instilled into her troubled
mind designs of no wider scope than this. The

---

[1] The other three were Sir Spencer Compton, who as Lord Wilmington
succeeded Walpole in 1742 ; Addington, who stepped directly from
Speakership to Premiership, in succession to Pitt in 1801 ; and William
Grenville, who was Speaker for a few months in 1789, and became Prime
Minister in the short-lived government of All the Talents in 1806. The
Duke of Wellington, according to Croker (ii. 164), proposed to Manners
Sutton that he should make a Tory government in 1831.

views of the new Parliament were very different.
They had no patience with schemes of moderation
and comprehension. " We are plagued here,"
Swift wrote to Stella, " with an October Club ;
that is, a set of above a hundred Parliament men
of the country, who drink October beer at home,
and meet every evening in a tavern near the
Parliament, to consult affairs and drive things
on to extremes against the Whigs, to call the old
Ministry to account, and get off five or six heads. . . .
The queen, sensible how much she was governed
by the late Ministry, runs a little into the other
extreme, and is jealous in that point, even of those
who got her out of the others' hands." (18th
February 1711.) Between the jealous murmurs
of these men of the October Club who wanted the
heads of their enemies, and the pertinacity of the
queen, who would not stir beyond the point first
marked out for her, Harley had a hard game to
play, and it soon appeared that he was not the
man to play it.

The savage and unholy genius of Swift had
appeared early on the scene. Exasperated at the
failure of his Whig friends to fulfil their promises
of church preferment, he had been willingly caught
by the attentions and the flatteries of the Tory
chiefs. " We were determined to have you," said
St. John. " You were the only one we were
afraid of." So they had him, his potent mind, his
virile and ingenious style, his irony, his penetration,
his truculence, his hate—all was henceforth at the
service of his new patrons. The history of polemical journalism records nothing more effective for
their purpose than the sallies for attack and for
defence made by Swift, along with Prior, Parnell,
and Defoe, against forces which counted Steele
and Addison. Never before nor since were so
many authors of classics which the world will not
willingly let die, engaged on ephemeral pieces

which the world willingly lets die on the next morning. Addison rose or fell from the ranks of letters to be a Secretary of State and a Cabinet minister, but his ascent was due to milder and happier gifts than those which led to the elevation of his friend. Never before nor since in England has a journalist, or a pamphleteer, achieved the position of personal ascendancy which was Swift's under the Tory administration of Queen Anne. He was a central figure at levees and drawing-rooms, and the hero of the ministers' ante-room. He was asked to Cabinet dinners, they called him Jonathan, he drove down to Windsor alone with Harley in his coach, he thought he was in all the secrets. In truth he was the dupe of his great friends. They told him as much as was necessary for his pamphlets and his articles, and they told him no more. He never knew, for instance, of Prior's clandestine mission to France, and to the very last he positively denied that there had been a whisper of intrigue with the court of St. Germains.

Swift tells how he dined with Bolingbroke and Harcourt at Harley's table in the infancy of their power, and he could not forbear taking notice of the affection they bore to one another. The first excitement of a new-made Cabinet is said to be singularly intoxicating. But it does not last. Swift speedily had the mortification of seeing this kindness between his friends first degenerate into indifference and suspicion, and then corrupt into the greatest animosity and hatred. The truth is evident from Swift's own accounts of Harley, in spite of the writer's strong and lasting partiality for him, that the Lord Treasurer had none of the gifts of a leader. He was hesitating, evasive, timid, promising what he did not perform, and full of repellent airs of discretion and reserve. Unlike Walpole afterwards, he had none of the stout and lively energy, none of the resolute and

imperious vigour, that was required to baffle the
spirit of intrigue and cabal in the royal closet and
his own Cabinet. His carelessness offended Mrs.
Masham, the queen's favourite. He allowed the
queen to become alienated and sullen, without
making an effort to remove the causes. He took
no pains to please his colleagues. His temper, he
once told Godolphin, was to go along with the
company and give no inconvenience. " If they
should say Harrow-on-the-Hill or by Maidenhead
were the nearest way to Windsor, I should go
with them, and never dispute it, if that would give
content, and that I might not be pressed to swear
it was so." This was true enough of his words, but
he forgot that though he would not dispute about
the road, in act he was always scheming to withdraw the lynch-pin and to upset the coach, and
his travelling companions knew it. The Whig
Lord Chancellor Cowper notes in his diary how
one day he was drinking healths with Harley in
some Tokay which was good but thick, and how
he said to Harley that his white Lisbon wine would
have been better, as being very clear. The company took it for a jest at " that humour of his,
which was never to deal clearly or openly, but
always with reserve if not dissimulation, or rather
simulation, and to love tricks where not necessary,
but from an inward satisfaction he took in ap-
plauding his own cunning. If any man was ever
born under a necessity of being a knave, he was."
Without going to such lengths as this, under the
ordeal of leadership his colleagues found out that
his moderation was a cloak for pusillanimity;
that his industry had sunk into the respectable
assiduity of a clerk ; that his self-possession was
no better than stolidity in disguise ; and that
all his airs of calculation, wisdom, and politic
reserve were only a blind to shifty dulness. He
was made angry and jealous by Bolingbroke's

intrepidity and despatch, for nothing is so irritating to a man who has much ambition with little industry, as the sight of energy and application in a real or a fancied rival. He soon presented to the world that most miserable of all sights, a minister called to direct great affairs, with the pitiful equipment of a mediocre judgment and a sluggish will. On the other hand, when the day of disgrace and peril came, Oxford showed both composure and courage. When his fall had become certain, Swift, notwithstanding grievances of his own against Oxford, praised him for fortitude and magnanimity, and maintained that he was the ablest and faithfullest minister and truest lover of his country that the age had produced.

The events of the last few months of the reign of Queen Anne from the autumn of 1713 to the summer of the following year, are a striking dramatic illustration of the trite moralities that spring from the vanity of human things. People assume that when men are concerned in high affairs, their motives must lie deep and their designs reach far. Few who have ever been close to public business, its hurries, chances, obscurities, egotisms, will fall in with any such belief. These very transactions draw from Swift the observation, so obvious, so useful, so constantly forgotten, what a lesson of humiliation it is to mankind to behold the habits and passions of men, otherwise highly accomplished, triumphing over interest, friendship, honour, and their own personal safety as well as that of their country. If St. John, for example, had been as sagacious and as honest as Walpole, he would never have left the House of Commons. His power and popularity in that assembly were immense, and he explained it in a famous sentence, which is perhaps as true of the House of Commons to-day as it was then. " Men there," he said, " grow, like hounds, fond

of the man who shows them game, and by whose
halloo they are used to be encouraged." The
common account of the two ministers is that
Oxford was a trifler and Bolingbroke a knave.
Bolingbroke's own theory was that Oxford had
no deep ambition and no policy beyond petty
objects of domestic aggrandisement, and he listened
with incredulous disgust while Oxford grew maudlin
over his claret in recounting the imaginary glories
of his ancestral house. Yet Bolingbroke, too,
must have been a trifler to quit the true scene
of authority for the sake of reviving the historic
honours of his family. He chose to desire the
title of an earl, partly because an earldom in his
name and family had lately become extinct, but
still more because Oxford had been raised to that
rank. This weak sacrifice of the substance of
power for the shadow of decoration, brought him
nothing but mischief. Swift had been called over
from Dublin in the summer of 1713 to try to compose their dissensions. He was almost the only
common friend who was left to them. Towards
the end of the year he thought he had done wonders
when he had contrived to get them to go to an
audience at Windsor together in the same coach,
without other company, and with four hours in
which to come to a good understanding. Two
days after he learned from them both that nothing
was done. Sometime in May (1714) Swift was
sitting with Oxford and Bolingbroke in Lady
Masham's apartment at St. James's, and after
some hours of talk called out to the Lord Treasurer
that, since he now despaired of a reconciliation
between them, he should leave London. Before
going he wished to ask them, first, whether these
mischiefs might not be remedied in two minutes ;
and next, whether on the present footing the
ministry would not be infallibly ruined in two
months. Bolingbroke said yes to both questions ;

but the Treasurer, "after his manner, evaded both, and only desired me to dine with him next day." Swift abruptly refused the dinner, and at once departed into Berkshire. There he remained until all was over. No domestic business was done, and no attention was paid to affairs abroad. Each day witnessed a new plot. The rivals seem to have respected neither themselves nor one another. Oxford and Bolingbroke continued to eat and drink and walk together as if no disagreement existed, and when they parted they used such names of one another as only politicians could have borne without cutting one another's throats. Even at the very end, the pair supped together at Lady Masham's after one of their most violent quarrels. It is almost incredible that ministers with such issues at stake, nursing serious purposes in their minds, and with the certainty of the crisis being close at hand, should have been capable of such lethargy and such levity.

The truth is that the game, as Swift called it, was too hard not only for Harley, but for all the rest of the dishonest band whom he had gathered around him. When the hour of crisis at last arrived, even Bolingbroke, daring and crafty as he seemed, was as much at sea as Harley had ever been. He wrote to Wyndham that nothing was more certain than that there was at this time no formed design in the party, whatever views some particular men might have, against the accession of King George. In the whole four years of his intimacy with ministers, Swift vows that he never heard one single word in favour of the Pretender. The entire imputation was nothing else but a device of Opposition. He often, he says, asked men in the Whig camp whether they did really suspect either the queen or her servants of having favourable regards towards the Pretender, and they all said no. More particularly one person,

afterwards in great employment, frankly told him,
"You set up the Church and Sacheverell against us,
and we set up Trade and the Pretender against you."

Yet it is now beyond all doubt that both Oxford
to a certain extent, and Bolingbroke very deeply,
were engaged in intrigues with the Pretender's
agents. Bolingbroke was quite aware of the desperate insecurity of a restoration policy. The
public was in as inconsistent a frame of mind as
either Oxford or Bolingbroke. As Lord Stanhope
has justly remarked, the country, with wonderful
blindness, resolutely adhered at the same time to
a Protestant king and to Jacobite ministers. They
prayed devoutly for the Electress Sophia, and
burnt in effigy the pope, the devil, and the Pretender ; yet they supported a Parliament that
suffered no step to be taken to the disadvantage
of· the most dangerous member of the trinity.
On the other hand, Bolingbroke saw that the
Hanoverian accession meant his own banishment
from power, and the final overthrow of his whole
Church and Tory policy. The Whigs had made
themselves absolutely indispensable to the House
of Hanover, as Hanover was to them. The only
course, if Bolingbroke and his friends were to retain
power, or to return to it, lay in a reconciliation
between them and the Elector, and reconciliation was impossible. Yet the statesman who had
mastered all the inextricable difficulties of Utrecht,
might be excused for dreaming that he was strong
enough and adroit enough to overcome even the
obstacles to a legitimist restoration.

In a sense it would be true to say that it was the
fidelity of the Tories to their Church that baulked
the legitimist plot, saved the Protestant succession,
and secured a parliamentary constitution. What
men like Swift, and the bulk of Tories more typical
than Swift, cared about was the Church. The
Church was to be preserved entire in all her rights,

powers, and privileges. All views on government condemned by her were to be discouraged by law, and all schisms and sects to be kept under due subjection. No dissenter of any denomination was to be trusted with the smallest degree of civil or military power; and no Whig, Low Churchman, republican, moderation man, or the like, was to receive any mark of favour from the Crown. Why should not the Hanoverians be induced to come into these views, and why should not ministers make terms with them? Why should not the young grandson of the Electress be invited over to be educated in England, to learn our manners and language, and to become acquainted with the true constitution in Church and State?

Such counsel might well have tempted anybody except the man who would have to execute it. Advice of this kind, which would be perfectly wise if only some vital condition happened to be totally different, is plenteously bestowed upon all party leaders in every generation. To make overtures to Hanover would be to give deadly offence to the queen, and to exasperate the Tory highfliers. It would be to run upon the rock that had wrecked Oxford, and in effect to throw away the most valuable weapon in the war against Oxford. Having no settled principles either way, and moved solely by personal ambition, Bolingbroke was driven towards Jacobitism by the nature of the political position. Whether Bolingbroke and Ormond were caballing with the agents of the Pretender merely with the view of procuring the dismissal of Oxford and making sure of Jacobite support, or were seriously aiming at a legitimist restoration, it was on either theory the urgent duty of the Whigs to exercise unsleeping vigilance. Happily for us they did not relax nor falter, and happily for Walpole the peril and distraction of that time made so deep a mark on his party, that almost

to the close of his career he always found a
potent argument for party fidelity at a pinch, in a
reminder of the last four years of Queen Anne.
The Tories pressed on their policy. They had
secured the Peace and destroyed Marlborough.
They had strengthened the landed interest by
the Act (1711) which required every knight of the
shire to have six hundred pounds a year from land,
and every burgess to have three hundred from
land. By a singularly disgraceful bargain between
some Whigs and the Tory malcontents of what
would now be called the Extreme Right, Parliament
had at length passed the bill against occasional
conformity. The Presbyterian could no longer
become the mayor of his town or the sheriff of his
county by a formal compliance with an invidious
test. This was not all. Bolingbroke, himself a
Deist or less, in conjunction with Atterbury, who
was a High Churchman and more, now crowned the
edifice of intolerance and exclusion by the Schism
Act, practically prohibiting the dissenters from
educating their own children. Walpole led a vehement resistance to this odious measure, but in vain.
The dissenters were thus prevented from keeping
public or private schools. They were shut out
from the universities. By the law against occasional conformity, they were shut out from the
corporations. If Bolingbroke could have had time
to deprive them of the parliamentary franchise, and
of the right of sitting in the House of Commons,
he would have completed his grand object. The
landed gentry and the Crown would have become
the possessors of supreme authority, and the
party system would have been extinguished by
the permanent instalment of one party in power.
The position was curiously like that of the Duke
de Broglie and the party of moral order and
Christian monarchy in 1873.
The end arrived with dramatic swiftness. The

D

favourite declared against Oxford; she told him roundly that he never had done the queen any service, and that he never would. The queen was slow to act. The fatal irresolution, said Boling-broke, which was inherent in the Stuart race, hung about her. At length her torpid will was roused, and she broke into bitter reproaches against the minister. On one of the last days of July (1714) an angry scene took place between Bolingbroke and Oxford in the very presence of the sovereign. The Lord Treasurer was commanded to deliver up the white staff of his office. He had been led to expect that his fall would be broken by a dukedom and a pension; he got neither, but was dismissed per-emptorily and with every circumstance of ignominy and mortification. But Bolingbroke's triumph was short. The queen, bewildered, stunned, and worn out by the animosity and confusion that raged around her, suffered an apoplectic seizure. For five days she lay at Kensington only half-conscious.

The country was in keen suspense, with all the omens of a rapidly approaching civil war. There was a revival of the temper of 1682, when the Whigs, in disgust at the actual oppressions of Charles II. and the threatened tyranny of James, had revolved plans of open rebellion, and prepared risings in arms at London, Bristol, and Newcastle. French refugee officers were ready to act under the orders of General Stanhope. Marlborough, then at Antwerp, was persuading the Dutch to send ships and men to aid the Protestant cause. He had made his preparations for an invasion, though it is doubtful whether he was not more likely to play the part of General Monk than of William the deliverer. In the Tory camp there was equal alertness. The military posts were manned by officers of the right principles. Bolingbroke pre-pared his list of appointments. He was for a government exclusively of Jacobites, including

Bishop Atterbury as Lord Privy Seal. The French minister says that Bolingbroke assured him that all his measures were so well taken, that within six weeks there would have been no fear of the result. Yet at this very moment he had a meeting at his house in Golden Square with Walpole, Pulteney, and Stanhope. When the moment of crisis arrived, he was still drifting. A gentleman came up post-haste from Cheshire. " Well, my lord," he said to Bolingbroke, " what is to be done ? " The eager partisan found his leader in a palsy of indecision.

The queen had no further part to play on the sublunary stage. The white staff had not yet been settled. On Friday, 30th July, the political committee of the Privy Council, sitting at the Cockpit at Whitehall, were summoned to Kensington by urgent representations of the queen's dangerous condition. While they were seated, two Whig peers, the Dukes of Argyll and Somerset, entered the room. As Privy Councillors they were within their technical right, though the fact of their using it shows how little the modern practice of the Cabinet was yet established. The physicians were summoned, and they reported that the queen's case was desperate. It was then agreed to recommend her to appoint the Duke of Shrewsbury to be Lord Treasurer. There is some reason for supposing that this step was taken on the proposition of Bolingbroke himself. He had perceived some time before that his character was too bad to carry the great ensign of power, but he felt that his ability would secure supreme authority whether with or without the wand. They approached the bedside of the dying sovereign. Rousing herself from her lethargy, she handed to Shrewsbury the white staff for which, or for the power of which it was the emblem, so many great men have been willing to barter away their souls. According to current story she handed it to him with the one regal utterance of her dismal life : she hoped that he would hold it for the good of her people. Another story is that as she lay dying, she uttered several times the hopeless cry of remorseful affection, " Oh, my brother, my dear brother ! " She only lived a day longer. " Sleep," wrote Arbuthnot to Swift, " was never more welcome to a weary traveller than death to her." To Swift also Bolingbroke wrote, two days after the cup had been dashed from his lips : " The Earl of Oxford was removed on Tuesday ; the queen died on Sunday. What a world is this, and how does fortune banter us." " It is true, my lord," replied Swift ; " the events of five days last week might furnish morals for another volume of Seneca." The artful fabric of policy and of party, in which all the crafty calculations, the fierce passions, the glowing hopes and confident ambitions of so many busy, powerful, and ardent minds had been for four years so eagerly concentrated, was in a single moment dashed to pieces. A century and a quarter elapsed before a queen again reigned over the British realm.

CHAPTER III

THE accession of the house of Hanover in the person of the great-grandson of James I. was once called by a Whig of this generation the greatest miracle in our history. It took place without domestic or foreign disturbance. Louis XIV. was now in his seventy-sixth year, and his orb was sinking over a weak, impoverished, and depopulated kingdom. Even he did not dare to expose himself to the hazards of a new war with Great Britain. Within our own borders a short lull followed the sharp agitations of the last six months. The new king appointed an exclusively Whig Ministry. The office of Lord Treasurer was not revived, and the title disappears from political history. Lord Townshend was made principal Secretary of State, and assumed the part of First Minister. Mr. Walpole took the subaltern office of Paymaster of the Forces, holding along with it the paymastership of Chelsea Hospital. Although he had at first no seat in the inner Council or Cabinet, which seems to have consisted of eight members, only one of them a commoner, it is evident that from the outset his influence was hardly second to that of Townshend himself. In little more than a year (October 1715) he had made himself so prominent and valuable in the House of Commons, that the opportunity of a vacancy was taken to appoint him to be First Commissioner of the Treasury and

Chancellor of the Exchequer. Lord Halifax and
Lord Carlisle had in turn preceded him in the
latter office. Since Walpole, save for a few months
after Stanhope accepted a peerage in 1717, and
before Aislabie succeeded him in 1718, the Chancellor
of the Exchequer has always been in the House
of Commons, a change that marked one further
stage in the growing ascendancy of the representative and the taxing chamber.

Historians have sometimes urged that Townshend and Walpole ought now to have advised
the king to bring a section of Tories into the
ministry. At that date, at any rate, a policy of
inclusion seems to have been practically out of
the question. Passion had risen to far too high
a degree of heat and violence to allow of the
composition of a mixed government, even if a
mixed government had been desirable. But in the
interest of the national settlement, nothing could
have been less desirable. A struggle for life and
death had just been brought to a good end, less by
design or concert than by the fortunate accident
of the demise of the Crown. It would have been
irrational to expect men who had only a few weeks
before been ready to resort to armed force against
one another, and who had just been risking their
estates and their heads on a great and decisive
issue, now at a moment's notice to sit down in
amity round the new king's council table. Even
if the Whig leaders had been free from personal
repugnance, and the Tory leaders had been willing
to come into the combination, it would have been
the height of infatuation to prepare to face wavering
Parliaments and a visibly approaching insurrection,
with a divided, lukewarm, or uncertain Cabinet.
Experience both before and after Walpole's era was
entirely adverse to mixed governments. William
III. tried it on two occasions, and each time it
was the judgment of the best observers that the

admission to place of men of doubtful allegiance only added to his troubles. Anne tried it from 1704 to 1708, and Marlborough and Godolphin found the failure complete. George II. tried it when Walpole had disappeared, and no attempt to make a strong government was less successful than that made on the principle of the Broad Bottom. If ever there was a time when comprehension, even on a small scale, would have been at once perilous and futile, it was the quarter of a century after the accession of the House of Hanover.

Besides excluding their opponents from power, the Whigs instantly took more positive measures. The new Parliament was strongly Whig. A secret committee was at once appointed to inquire into the negotiations for the Peace. Walpole was chairman, took the lead in its proceedings, and drew the report. The topics of the report were such as at the present day would figure in a motion of censure. They are a recapitulation of all the objections to be urged against the terms of the Peace. Every objection was supported by extracts from authentic documents. Walpole took five hours in reading the report to the House, and the clerk at the table read it over again on the following day. It is a great political indictment, charging the queen's ministers with deserting their allies and betraying the honour and the interests of the realm. The only truly criminal part of the accusation, that which related to secret transactions with the Pretender, breaks down, and was felt to have broken down. The intrigue was undoubted, but the intriguers and their confederates had been too discreet to leave dangerous papers behind in their desks. The evidence that would have condemned them was then hidden in the despatch-boxes at St. Germains.

Impeachment, however, was still naturally regarded as the proper process against ministers who had gravely offended a triumphant majority. It was the only way then known of securing responsibility to Parliament. A Tory House in 1701 impeached Somers, Halifax, Oxford, and Portland, for the part they had taken in the Spanish Partition Treaties of 1700. A Whig House now (1715) directed the impeachment of Oxford, Bolingbroke, and Ormond for high treason, and other high crimes and misdemeanours mainly relating to the Peace of Utrecht. When Walpole himself fell, a generation later (1742), there was a loud and sanguinary cry that he should be impeached. But even by that time this way of striking a political delinquent was beginning to seem anomalous. The proceedings against Oxford and Bolingbroke are the last instance in our history of a political impeachment. They are the last ministers who were ever made personally responsible for giving bad advice and pursuing a discredited policy, and since then a political mistake has ceased to be a crime. Warren Hastings was impeached (1788), and so was Lord Melville (1804), but neither case was political, for Hastings was charged with misgovernment, and Melville with malversation of official funds. Burke said in 1770 that impeachment was dead, even to the very idea of it, and later history has shown that he was substantially in the right. The explanation of the disappearance of this old political expedient is twofold. A refinement in men's sense of equity gradually disclosed the hardship of punishing ministers for acts that Parliament and the sovereign had approved ; and second, the remarkable growth of the Cabinet system, of which I shall have something to say on a later page, tended slowly but decisively to substitute the joint responsibility of the whole body of ministers for the personal responsibility of an individual minister. To impeach, or to pass an Act either of attainder or of pains and penalties against, a whole Cabinet would be practically absurd and impossible.

Walpole's share in pressing for these strong measures against his fallen enemies is matter of some doubt. Bolingbroke charges him with being their hottest advocate. There is no positive evidence either way. Walpole was a man of humane and moderate temper, but he was by no means a man averse to strike if he thought a blow required. Though he had no rancour by nature, he knew how to be relentless as a matter of business. He had been the leader in sifting the evidence before his secret committee. When somebody prophesied that the committee would end in smoke, Walpole vehemently cried out that he wanted words to express his sense of the villainy of the late Frenchified ministry. To us, to whom impeachment is almost as much of an antiquity as ordeal by fire, and in whom the Treaty of Utrecht excites only historic interest and no passion, the whole proceeding may seem intemperate and impolitic. Yet a cool and sagacious bystander may very easily have thought differently. The country was in many parts unsettled. The proclamation of King George had been in some places attended by riot and disorder. The Church was violent against the House of Hanover. London was so uncertain that, for long after the accession, cannon were kept at Whitehall to keep the mob in awe. The Highlanders were rising. It was in conformity to the political notions of the time, as it is to those of our own time in relation to Ireland, to strike vindictive blows of this kind. Such considerations as these may well have had their weight in the ministerial decision. The affair came to an abortive end. After Oxford had lain a year in the Tower, it was resolved to reduce the charges against him from high treason to misdemeanour; and after another year a difference arose, or was promoted by

Walpole's connivance, between the Lords and the Commons as to the mode of procedure. After a prolonged exchange of explanations, the Commons resolved to drop the prosecution (1717).

The opening years of the new reign mark one of the least attractive periods in political history. George I. was silent, simple, and not ill-meaning; he was attentive to business, thrifty, and pacific. He had some ambition to play a high and stately part, if he had only known how. But he cared very little for his new kingdom, and knew very little about its people or its institutions. He brought over with him a couple of rapacious mistresses and a swarm of courtiers, eager for the milk and honey of the promised land. It is not surprising that violent feuds should have speedily arisen between this crew of greedy strangers and the home-bred minister from Norfolk. Walpole coarsely said of Schulenberg, afterwards Duchess of Kendal, the elder of the two royal favourites, that she was of so venal a nature that she would have sold the king's honour for a shilling advance to the highest bidder. The spirit of jobbery was insatiable. The office of Master of the Horse was left vacant, and the duchess received the salary. No Master of the Buckhounds was appointed : the emolument went into a German pocket. When Walpole remonstrated with the king against these outrageous venalities, the king with a smile replied in the bad Latin in which, as neither of them knew the language of the other, he and his minister were said to converse together : " I suppose that you are also paid for your recommendations."

The manners of the outlandish invaders were as bad as their morals. One of them once carried his insolence so far that Walpole, though he was in the royal presence, summoning both the Latin and the frankness that he had learned at Eton, cried out to the offender, " *Mentiris impudentissime.*"

His worst enemy was Robethon, the king's French secretary. " This man," said Walpole, " —a mean fellow, of what nation I know not—having obtained the grant of a reversion, which he designed for his son, I thought it too good for him, and therefore reserved it for my own son. On this disappointment the foreigner impertinently demanded £2500, under pretence that he had been offered that sum for the reversion, but I was wiser than to comply with his demands." Townshend was equally resolute in resisting the importunities of the two favourite ladies for English peerages, for reversions, grants, and all the rest of the perquisites which the Hanoverians regarded as their rightful spoil. The inevitable result was the growth of a bitter enmity in the minds of the king's favourite advisers and companions, and its gradual transfusion into the mind of the king himself.

Another source of danger to ministers sprang up within. Rival ambitions began to appear in the Whig camp almost as soon as the administration was formed. Townshend and Walpole stood together. They came from the same county, they had been at the same school, and Townshend had married Walpole's sister. Like Walpole, Townshend was a solid man, apt in business, assiduous, and firm, but unlike Walpole in being hot, impulsive, and impatient. The elevation of the two new ministers is said to have given umbrage to the ambition of Sunderland. His contemporaries could not agree whether the third Earl of Sunderland was quite so bad a man as his father, the faithless and unprincipled minister of James II. He hid violent passions under an austere and frigid demeanour; he sought no friends, and he affected to regard books as the only worthy companions of lofty natures. He formed an important collection of early and rare editions of the Greek and Latin classics at Althorp, destined in a later generation to become the home of still nobler and more splendid treasures. Sunderland fell short of money, and with a pang that none but a bibliomaniac can know, he transferred his beloved books for a sum of ten thousand pounds to his father-in-law, the Duke of Marlborough, in whose hands they became the foundation of the great Blenheim Library, dispersed not many years ago. Among other effects of Sunderland's classical reading, it had made him a fiery republican. He even thought fit to entertain Queen Anne with injurious reflections on the wickedness of princes. Sunderland was clever, busy, and persevering, and he was thought to be the greatest intriguer since his father. He was described besides as being "not only the most intriguing, but the most passionate man of his time." Walpole was once asked why he never came to an understanding with Sunderland. "You little know Lord Sunderland," he replied. "If I had so much as hinted at it, his temper was so violent that he would have done his best to throw me out of the window." Something deeper, however, than temper divided the Sunderland Whigs from Walpole. Aristocratic pride in union with republican professions has often produced the narrowest type of oligarch; and Sunderland's republicanism only meant that the wings of royal prerogative were to be clipped for the benefit of a small caste of exclusive patricians. He hated the Crown, but he had none of Walpole's respect and inclination for the Commons. It was no wonder that they soon fell out.

Walpole once remarked how difficult it is to trace the causes of a dispute between statesmen. Some transactions of our own day furnish a striking illustration of the truth of this remark, and the difficulty of explaining such disputes would be most readily admitted by those who might seem to hold the clue. Walpole's biographer maintains

that it was Sunderland's discontent and Stanhope's
weakness and bad faith that lay at the bottom of
the Whig schism of 1717. Stanhope's descendant,
the careful historian of those times, insists that
the rupture was due to Townshend's unreasonable-
ness and want of judgment. It is not possible at
this distance of time, and with imperfect material,
conclusively to settle the question. The king
hated his son, and the Prince of Wales was bent
on making a party of his own against his father.
The foreigners hated the English ministers, and
the ministers were stubbornly set against the demands of the foreigners. The Cabinet was divided
by no serious dissent on principle or policy, but
by the even more dangerous element of personal
jealousy and dissatisfied ambition. All these conditions united to make schism inevitable.

The king left his new dominion for Hanover
in July 1716. His passion for his native land,
like his ignorance of the tongue of the land that
had adopted him, was a piece of good fortune
for constitutional government. His inability to
speak English led to that important change in
usage, the absence of the sovereign from Cabinet
Councils. His expeditions to Hanover threw the
management of all domestic affairs almost without
control into the hands of his English ministers.
If the first two Hanoverian kings had been Englishmen instead of Germans, if they had been men of
talent and ambition, or even men of strong and
commanding will without much talent, Walpole
would never have been able to lay the foundations
of government by the House of Commons and by
Cabinet so firmly that even the obdurate will of
George III. was unable to overthrow it. Happily
for the system now established, circumstances compelled the first two sovereigns of the Hanoverian
line to strike a bargain with the English Whigs,
and it was faithfully kept until the accession of the

third George. The king was to manage the affairs
of Hanover, and the Whigs were to govern England.
It was an excellent bargain for England.

Smooth as this operation may seem in historic
description, Walpole found its early stages rough
and thorny. The first royal visit to the electoral
dominions speedily brought to light the perils that
lay alike in the hatred between father and son,
and in the rivalry among ministers. The double
leaven soon began to work. The Hanoverians
played upon the king's jealousy of the prince,
and rapidly instilled into his mind the suspicion
that Townshend and his colleagues were intriguing
with Argyll and the prince's party in England.
It is as certain as anything can be in matters so
obscure and intricate, that for this charge there
was no foundation, and that Walpole was justified
in assuring Stanhope, with wholesome bluntness,
that whoever sent over the accounts of any intrigues
of this kind, or any management in the least tend-
ing to any view or purpose but the service, honour,
and interest of the king, would be discovered
to be " confounded liars from the beginning to
the end."

Nor was it possible to cut off the politics of
Hanover from the politics of Great Britain. The
acquisition of Bremen and Verden from Sweden
for the electorate of Hanover, was approved by
Walpole on the ground that the two provinces
commanded the only inlets from British waters
into Germany. They secured the trade with
Hamburg, and put a check on the molestation by
Sweden of British commerce in the Baltic. When
the king, however, for Hanoverian reasons sought
to make war on the Czar of Russia, because he
had invaded the Grand Duchy of Mecklenburg,
Townshend declared that the nation would never
consent to make sacrifices for interests that were
none of theirs, and Walpole vowed that he could

not raise the money. The king was furious, and his exasperation at being thwarted in his warlike designs was artfully inflamed by hints that the ministers in England were secretly striving to exalt the Prince of Wales, and to show that the business of Parliament could be as well transacted by the son as by the father.

A pretext was found for the removal of Townshend from his office, in circumstances which it is not worth while here to recapitulate. They would never have been deemed adequate cause for so strong a step, if other motives had not operated, and it is impossible to acquit either Sunderland or Stanhope of singular disloyalty to their friends and colleagues in London. Walpole had described the situation in a private letter to Stanhope at Hanover : " The prince hates us, and at the same time we are almost lost with the king, having all the foreigners determined against us." Even the loosest form in which we can imagine the great and honourable conception of loyalty among members of a Cabinet, as it is now held, would condemn the action of the two ministers at Hanover in lending themselves to the king's designs against absent colleagues. In the sharp recriminations that were exchanged between Stanhope and Walpole, the former takes up ground with which it is impossible to feel satisfied. Was he, Stanhope asks, to tell the king that Townshend must continue to be Secretary of State, or else that the Whigs would quit office in a body ? " I really have not yet learnt to speak such language to my master ; and I think a king is very unhappy if he is the only man in the nation who cannot challenge any friendship from those of his subjects whom he thinks fit to employ." It will be observed that the question raised by Stanhope touches an essential part of Cabinet government. Is the king to exercise unfettered choice in the distribution or redistribution of offices ? Even if we assume that they are taken exclusively from one party, is he to command the services of individual leaders at his own discretion, and to assign them their respective offices as to him may seem good ? Queen Anne had undoubtedly acted on this principle. Walpole thought that the time had come for ministers to settle their offices among themselves.

Townshend was prevailed upon for a very short time to remain in the administration as Lord-Lieutenant of Ireland, then always a Cabinet office. But the truce did not last. The king's favour had too evidently gone to Sunderland and Stanhope. On the proposal that the Commons should vote supplies for preparations against Sweden, the Townshend Whigs showed themselves cold and disaffected ; Walpole spoke coldly for the vote, but lent it no active support ; and it was only carried by a majority of four. In his resentment at this narrow escape of a government measure, the king dismissed Townshend from his post the same night. Walpole was too valuable at the Treasury to be so lightly parted with. Vain attempts were made to separate him from his colleague. The tender of his resignation the next morning was followed by an extraordinary scene in the royal closet. The king entreated him not to retire, and put the seals back into his hat. Walpole protested that if as Chancellor of the Exchequer he found money for the warlike designs of Stanhope and Sunderland, he would lose his credit and reputation ; and if, on the other hand, he resisted them, then he would forfeit the gracious favour of his sovereign. No fewer than ten times were the seals replaced upon the table. The king at length gave way, and Walpole quitted the closet with tears in his eyes, leaving his master as painfully agitated as himself.

There was one quarter in which the split in the

Whig party and the fierce quarrel in the royal
family stirred the liveliest delight. Atterbury,
the conspirator who then held the episcopal see of
Rochester, was now, under elaborate disguise of
cypher and cant names, writing to the Pretender
sanguine accounts of what was going on at court.
From these letters we learn how high the Jacobite
hopes were raised by the removal of the two
ministers who were well known to be the fastest
friends of the present settlement. Every piece of
gossip about the dissensions between the Prince
of Wales and the Duke of Hanover, as they styled
King George, was magnified into a reason for the
fond belief, which only the inveterate fatuity of
plotters in exile could have entertained, that the
king would rather throw the British crown to the
Pretender than suffer it to devolve on his detested
heir. Every movement of the public funds sent
their spirits up or down, as if they were bears
on a stock exchange. The Tories were as elated
as the pure Jacobites. They flattered themselves
that the Whigs were so divided, that nothing
short of another rebellion could bring them together
again. The city Whigs, ignorant of the personal
intrigues behind the scenes, and bewildered by such
rapid changes in administration, were all anxiety
to know what they could mean.

The truth is that the Whigs were in so great
a majority that, like all parties in such circumstances, they could afford moderate quarrels among
themselves. The famous Septennial Act of 1716
had secured their parliamentary majority for some
years to come. It had once been among the prerogatives of the Crown to retain the same Parliament during the life of the sovereign, and Charles
II. did actually keep the Cavalier Parliament for
seventeen years. Such excess produced reaction,
and in 1694 Parliament passed an Act limiting its
normal lifetime to periods of three years. In 1716

E

the great exigencies of the time justified a move
in the other direction, and an extension of the life
of a Parliament from three years to seven. The
measure, which was originally designed for the
special object of securing the Protestant succession
at a moment of peril, had wider consequences.
Speaker Onslow, the sage observer of parliamentary
events, used to declare that the Septennial Bill of
1716 marked the true era of the emancipation of
the House of Commons from its former dependence
on the Crown and the House of Lords.[1] The Act
was undoubtedly one of the most important causes
of the increase of that power in the House of
Commons, on which Walpole was the first minister
habitually and on principle to rely. Meanwhile it
enabled the Whigs in 1717 to cut themselves in two
with impunity.

After leaving court in 1717, Walpole remained
in opposition for three years. Many blamed him
for deserting the king. Many declared that it was
desertion of the country and of Parliament to
abandon schemes for reducing the national debt,
which, as he was well aware, no successor had the
ability to carry through. Walpole protested, as
so many men since have protested in the same
circumstances, that nothing was further from his
mind than to embarrass government. But when
men leave colleagues in a government, they seldom
see how far their departure may lead them. The
spirit of party, and the restlessness of a powerful
nature, were too strong for the practice of benevolent
neutrality. While loudly disclaiming any desire
to embarrass the king's ministers, he still found
himself invariably compelled bitterly to resist all
their measures. He opposed the Mutiny Bill,
though its provisions were merely formal and were
necessary. He opposed the repeal of the Schism
Act, though he had himself once denounced it as

[1] Coxe, i. 137.

more worthy of Julian the Apostate than of the Protestant Parliament of England. So apt is party spirit to degenerate into moral paradox.

Yet none of these excesses or inconsistencies shook his hold on Parliament. Nor is that hold hard to understand. To begin with, he showed upon occasion the moderating temper which the House of Commons always secretly respects, even in its moments of passion and of heat, and which it always recognises when the heat has evaporated. A member had greatly offended the House, by bringing against a certain set of men that charge of obstruction which has become part of the common form of party scolding in later days. A few words from Walpole were enough to save the gentleman from being sent to the Tower. Shippen, the Jacobite leader, said of the king's speech that it seemed rather calculated for the meridian of Germany than of Great Britain, and regretted his Majesty's ignorance of our language and our constitution. The House was furious at this uncourtly plainness, but Walpole composed the angry waves, and " honest Shippen " would easily have escaped, if his honesty had not taken the form, as honesty sometimes does, of obstinate contumacy. But the true basis of Walpole's power was something more positive than a moderating temper. He was a skilful manager of men, but he was also an unrivalled man of business. Wherever money was concerned, his knowledge, skill, clearness, and judgment gave him an authority that was paramount. In all these transactions, even his worst enemies had with mortification to admit that the House of Commons relied more upon Walpole's opinion than upon that of any other member. In weighing the ordinary accusation that his immense parliamentary influence was due to gross corruption, it is well not to forget that he laid the foundations of that influence while he was in opposition and without strong party support, and without any of the means of corruption. The truth is that the House of Commons has always been most wisely ready to give its confidence to men whom it believes to possess a firm, broad, and independent grasp of the great material interests of the country.

The time was close at hand when neglect of Walpole's practical wisdom brought upon the nation a terrible disaster. Before this catastrophe arrived, Walpole was provoked to the exertion of all his powers by a proposal of the gravest constitutional moment. Sunderland was in extreme disfavour with the Prince of Wales, and he was well aware that the death of the reigning king would at once lead to his own dismissal. The centre of gravity was still in the Upper House, where the Whigs had a standing majority : the prince's first step, therefore, on coming to the throne would be to strengthen the Tory minority in the House of Lords. Queen Anne had set him a precedent in the creation of the twelve peers to carry the Peace of Utrecht. That this was a violent act, honest Tories admitted, but they declared that, after all, it was not to be compared with the act by which the Commons, chosen by the people for three years, chose themselves for seven. Sunderland did not shrink from taking an audacious measure to counterwork the danger in advance. Lord Stanhope was made to bring in a bill for putting a close restriction on the royal prerogative of making peers. The number of peers, according to the bill, was never at any time to be enlarged beyond six over the number then existing. At the accession of George I. the total number of the peers, including the twenty-six peers spiritual and the sixteen representative peers from Scotland, was two hundred and seven.[1]

---

[1] At the accession of William IV. the number, including the addition of thirty-two temporal and spiritual peers from Ireland, had risen to three hundred and ninety. (Stanhope's *History of England*, ch. ii. 44.)

Instead of the sixteen elective members from Scotland, twenty-five from that kingdom were to be made hereditary. Where a failure of issue male occurred, it might be filled up by new creation in England, and by selection from other members of the peerage in Scotland. Obviously, if such a measure had become law, it would have transformed the House of Lords into a close college, and the peerage would have become an unchangeable caste. The Lords would have acquired a fixed preponderance of power over Crown and Commons alike ; for while the Crown could coerce the Commons by a dissolution, and the Commons could restrain the Crown by refusal of supplies, the Lords would have been beyond the reach of either of the other two branches of the legislature.

That this far-reaching measure failed to become law, is due to Walpole's penetration and rapidity, and by hardly any other action of his life did he set a deeper stamp upon our system of government. Formidable difficulties were in his way. The king might have been expected to object to a limitation of one of the most cherished of royal prerogatives. But the king hated the Prince of Wales, and was as anxious as Sunderland to clip his wings. The Scotch peers were won by the prospect of exchanging an elective for a hereditary seat. The Lords as a whole were openly or privately gratified by a measure which, in limiting their numbers, augmented their individual importance. The bill engaged the talents of the two most delightful prose writers of the day. It was defended by Addison, in what proved to be the final task of his life, and it was attacked by Steele. Why could not faction, says Johnson, find other advocates ? " Controvertists cannot long retain their kindness for each other, and every reader must surely regret that these two illustrious friends, after so many years passed in confidence and endearment,

in unity of interest, conformity of opinion, and
fellowship of study, should finally part in acrimonious opposition." The spirit of faction was
too busy and too hot for these pensive regrets, and
no effort was spared to forward the ministerial
design. The king's name was freely used. Sunderland told everybody that the king wished the bill ;
that the Prince of Wales would otherwise do mad
things when he came to the throne ; that if the
Whigs rejected it, their party would be for ever
undone. Bribes and threats were employed with
equal profusion. All this took the heart out of
the Opposition Whigs. They held a meeting at
Devonshire House, where Walpole found them
lukewarm, indifferent, and out of spirits. He at
once took a high tone, protested against any weakness, and used all the topics that are the common
property in all ages of all militant leaders of Opposition pressing sluggish adherents to make a fight.
Public opinion, he said, was rising against the
bill. The country gentlemen were waking up to
the insult implied upon their class by a measure
which would shut the door of the House of Lords
in their faces. He had himself overheard a country
gentleman with not more than eight hundred
pounds a year, vow with great warmth to another
country gentleman, that though he had no chance
of being made a peer himself, he would never
consent to lay his family under the ban of perpetual
exclusion. Finally, he used the universal and irresistible clencher that it was a splendid opportunity
of weakening and discrediting the government.
" Even if I am deserted by my party," he said,
winding up his animated remonstrance, " I myself
will singly stand forth and oppose it." A lively
altercation followed, but such high and inspiriting
firmness in a political leader with an accepted
character for judgment, is always sure to carry the
day. The party came over to Walpole's opinion,

and he further justified it by a speech whose qualities the historian does not overrate in declaring it to be one of the most eloquent and masterly ever delivered in the House of Commons, whether we judge it by impressions of the time, or by the effect of the report of it upon our own minds.[1]

There is nothing in it comparable to that superb passage in which the greatest writer of the century in its last decade defended a natural aristocracy.[2] Nevertheless it is an excellent setting for what a first-rate judge of a later day used to describe as the very best parliamentary argument he knew, excepting Mr. Gladstone's speech on the taxation of charities. Walpole's reasoning, and the energy with which it was urged, led to the rejection of the bill by a triumphant majority of two hundred and sixty-nine against one hundred and seventy-seven.

[1] This famous speech is given in outline by Coxe, ch. xviii.
[2] *Appeal from the New to the Old Whigs*, p. 217 (ed. 1818).

CHAPTER IV

To the great dismay of the Jacobites, the two circumstances on which they had been so fondly counting suddenly took a new turn. The Whig schism came to an end, and the king allowed himself to be reconciled to his son. Walpole played an active part in both of these transactions. As clearly as the Jacobites, he perceived that the feud between the prince and the king threatened real dangers to the peace of the realm. Things had reached such a pitch that the king actually consulted the Lord Chancellor as to the legality of a bill for compelling the Prince of Wales, on the demise of the Crown, to divest himself of his German dominions. A much more sinister project was found among the king's papers at his death, nothing less than a proposal made by the head of the Admiralty to seize the Prince of Wales and carry him off to the wilds of America. This atrocious design recalls the old rumour that Buckingham had offered to oblige Charles II. by kidnapping his consort, despatching her to some colony, and then grounding a divorce on the plea of wilful desertion. Notwithstanding his hatred of his son, and his grim usage of his unfortunate wife, George I. was not the man to listen to a scheme of this kind. When Walpole at last prevailed upon the prince to send his father a submissive message, it was graciously received ; the letter was followed by a visit to the king at St. James's, and to show that he and the sovereign were once more on terms, the prince was sent back to his house in Leicester Fields with a complimentary escort of life guards.

Walpole's return to the administration was part of the same political scheme, just as his fall twenty years later was connected with the position of the heir apparent of that day. A man of his energy and passion for the work of government is apt to grow tired of opposition, and public considerations pointed in the same way as his own ruling impulse. The end of the Whig schism involved a general closing up of ranks in face of new alarms from the Pretender. The reunion of the Whigs was at least as welcome to the men in office as to the men in opposition. The hand that had just destroyed the Peerage Bill was too heavy to be left with safety outside the government. Yet though Walpole and Townshend once more joined the administration, they were forced to content themselves with subordinate posts. Townshend, who had filled what was then the leading office of Secretary of State, became Lord President of the Council; and Walpole, who had been First Lord of the Treasury and Chancellor of the Exchequer, was made Paymaster of the Forces without a seat in the Cabinet (1720). His opposition was at an end, but he took no part in the active work of government, and in the summer withdrew to Norfolk to bide his time.

Before many months had passed the country was overtaken by the memorable disasters of the South Sea Bubble. This famous project, which was indirectly the means of Walpole's ascendancy, had its origin in the same delusions about the fabulous wealth of Spanish America that twenty years later led to the Spanish War and to Walpole's fall. France had been thrown into a frenzy of speculation by the Mississippi schemes of Law.

The fever quickly spread to England, with a difference that may be worth noting, that while Law was a man of genius and by no means without sincerity and even elevation of character, in London the promoters were little more than ordinary stock-jobbers with extraordinary rashness, audacity, and corruption. The South Sea Act of 1720 was a measure for enabling the South Sea Company to absorb in their stock a quantity of irredeemable annuities, consolidate various branches of the public debt, reduce the rate of interest, and out of the profits of their trade eventually achieve one of the most eagerly desired objects of that day by paying off the national debt. Fortunately for himself, Walpole had at a very early stage exposed the fallacies on which the plan of the directors rested, though he remained an inactive colleague of ministers who were its zealous supporters. Thousands of bubble projects have been launched since that memorable mania, and early in the nineteenth century speculation in railway stock was almost as extravagant, widespread, and desperate as the great fever of 1721. But the South Sea scheme is in our history the only case of this ruinous calamity at which a government directly and actively connived. When the crash came, a cry broke out for vengeance, as fierce and as indiscriminate as outcries usually are, when people are bent on punishing others for their own blindness and folly. One peer in his place demanded that, in the absence of any adequate penalty by existing law, the South Sea directors should be treated like parricides in ancient Rome, stitched up in sacks, and flung into the river ; and on this occasion the peer was representative of the general judgment. Apart from the social confusion, the political danger was by no means slight. The German mistresses were known to have had a share in the spoil, the Prince of Wales had been chairman of a bubble

copper company from which he extracted forty
thousand pounds in a metal more precious than
copper; and besides these specific grounds for
anger, the natural tendency to blame government
was especially strong when that government was
new, foreign, unsettled, and unpopular.

All eyes were turned to Walpole. Though he
had privately dabbled in South Sea stock on his
own account, his public predictions came back
to men's minds; they remembered that he had
been called the best man for figures in the House,
and the disgrace of his most important colleagues
only made his sagacity the more prominent. Craggs,
the Secretary of State, and his father, the Postmaster-General, were both implicated in the receipt
of enormous sums, as the differences on transactions
in fictitious stock created to buy the passing of
the South Sea Bill. The son died of smallpox,
and the father quickly followed, leaving a fortune
of a million and a half. Aislabie, the Chancellor
of the Exchequer, was down for nearly eight
hundred thousand pounds, fraudulently acquired.
Sunderland was charged with similar transactions,
but whatever substance there may have been in
the charge, they had been managed discreetly
enough to leave a colourable excuse for acquitting
him. Still public opinion made it impossible for
Sunderland to retain office. Lord Stanhope, his
principal colleague, was removed by a curiously
sudden death in February 1721. In the course
of an angry debate, the young Duke of Wharton
compared Stanhope to Sejanus, the wicked minister
who fomented divisions in the imperial family,
and made the reign of Tiberius, his master, odious
to the Roman people. Stanhope was so incensed
at gibes that Walpole would only have laughed at,
that in the angry transport of his reply he was
seized with a fit, and the next day he expired.
This brought about a recasting of the ministerial

parts, and at the request of the great territorial Whigs, Walpole undertook the task. He returned to his old posts, and once more became First Lord of the Treasury and Chancellor of the Exchequer (April 1721), while Townshend was again Secretary of State.

Walpole held his offices practically without a break for twenty-one years. The younger Pitt had an almost equal span of unbroken supremacy, but with that exception there is no parallel to Walpole's long tenure of power. To estimate aright the vast significance of this extraordinary stability, we must remember that the country had just passed through eighty years of revolution. A man of eighty in 1721 could recall the execution of Charles I., the Protectorate of Oliver, the fall of Richard Cromwell, the restoration of Charles II., the exile of James II., the change of the order of succession to William of Orange, the reactionary ministry of Anne, and finally the second change to the House of Hanover. The interposition, after so long a series of violent perturbations as this, of twenty years of settled system and continuous order under one man, makes Walpole's government of capital and decisive importance in our history, and constitutes not an artificial division like the reign of a king, but a true and definite period, with a beginning, an end, a significance, and a unity of its own.

Parliamentary government has been said to prevent great shocks, but to multiply small ones. From the critical state of the time Walpole was ceaselessly exposed to these small shocks, and the vigour with which he circumvented the cabals that from the first year to the last surrounded and confronted him, was only less important to the security of the great public bulwark of his power, than the success with which he surmounted grave difficulties of state. It would have been easy for Walpole in South Sea affairs to avenge old griev-

ances on Sunderland and others. As it was he
chose the magnanimous course of insisting, even
at the expense of much unpopularity for himself,
on the most lenient counsels that Parliament
could be persuaded to allow. But the jealous and
unquiet Sunderland, even in the hour of his disgrace, was again busy on devices for displacing
the new rival in the royal favour. He hit upon the
extraordinary expedient of suggesting to the king
that he should create Walpole Postmaster-General
for life. His calculation was that the large pay
would tempt a man of narrow fortune; that if
Walpole accepted, he would be incapable of sitting
in Parliament; while, if he refused, he would offend
the king. The king, however, baulked the childish
plan by asking whether Walpole desired the proposal or knew of it. Sunderland confessed that
he did not. "Then," said the king, "do not make
him the offer. I parted with him once against my
inclination, and I will never part with him again,
so long as he is willing to serve me."

The king may well have felt the perilous situation from which Walpole's capacity had rescued
him. The discovery of the plot for which Atterbury
was exiled (1722), revealed how high Jacobite
hopes had risen during the recent confusion. In
the excitement some measures were taken with
Walpole's approval, which it is hard to justify.
The bill of pains and penalties against Atterbury
himself was a dangerous invasion of the security
and sanctity of legal guarantees, and it is satisfactory to think that it is the last instance of its
kind. Walpole appeared as a witness in the course
of the proceedings; the bishop used all his skill to
perplex his opponent; but, says Speaker Onslow,
he was too hard for the bishop at every turn,
"although a greater trial of skill this way scarce
ever happened between two such combatants."[1]

[1] Coxe, *Original Papers*, i. 328.

Still more alien, not only to the temper of to-day, but even to the better mind of that age, as Onslow's censures prove, was the imposition of a tax of £100,000 on Roman Catholics as a composition for recusancy, and it was presently extended even to non-jurors. "The whole nation almost, men, women, and children capable of taking an oath, flocked to the places where the quarter sessions were holden. . . . It was a strange as well as a ridiculous sight to see people crowding to give a testimony of their allegiance to a government, and cursing them at the same time for giving them the trouble of so doing and for the fright they were put into by it; and I am satisfied more real disaffection to the king and his family arose from it than from anything which happened at that time."—(Onslow). The lesson was not lost upon the minister; for no administration of the century, least of all that which closed the century, exhibited less of the spirit of oppression and intolerance.

Sunderland died in 1722, and left as his representative in the public counsels a statesman whose name has long ago faded away from general recollection, and who made no great mark on national policy, but yet was by the common consent of contemporaries unsurpassed by any man of his age in brilliance of gifts, compass of view, and aspiring vigour of character. Carteret was by far the ablest and most striking representative of the principles, policy, and temper in handling public business, that were most directly antagonistic to the principles, policy, and temper of Walpole. "He was a fine person," says Shelburne, who married his daughter, "of commanding beauty, the best Greek scholar of the age, overflowing with wit, not so much a *diseur de bons mots*, as a man of true, comprehensive, ready wit, which at once saw to the bottom, and whose imagination never failed him, and was joined to great natural

elegance. He had a species of oratory more calculated for the senate than the people."[1] It was
Carteret who said to Henry Fox, " I want to instil
a noble ambition into you ; to make you knock
the heads of the kings of Europe together, and
jumble something out of it that may be of service
to this country." " What is it to me," he once
said, "who is a judge or who is a bishop ? It is
my business to make kings and emperors, and
to maintain the balance of Europe." He was all
for glory, says Onslow, and thought much more
of raising a great name to himself all over Europe,
and having that continued by historians to all
posterity, than of any present domestic popularity
or renown whatever. A story is told of Carteret
which every lover of scholarship as a fine adorn-
ment of greatness in character or action, will
always delight to remember. As he lay dying
(1762) the Under-Secretary took to him, as Lord
President, the preliminary articles of the Treaty
of Paris. He found the minister so languid, that
he proposed to put off the business until another
day. Carteret replied by repeating the beautiful
lines, where Sarpedon says to Glaucus that if
keeping back from the fray would keep back age
and death from them, then indeed neither would
he himself fight amid the foremost, nor send the
other into the battle ; " but now — since ten
thousand shapes of death hover over us, and them
no mortal may escape—now, forward let us go."[2]

---

[1] *Shelburne's Life*, i. 38. Disraeli, who had brooded much over
Bolingbroke's period and his ideas, has some interesting remarks on
Carteret and Shelburne in *Sybil*, ch. iii. Oddly enough, while talking of
Carteret, the novelist says that Bolingbroke was the only peer of his
period who was educated. What of Chesterfield, too ?

[2] ὦ πέπον, εἰ μὲν γὰρ πόλεμον περὶ τόνδε φυγόντε
αἰεὶ δὴ μέλλοιμεν ἀγήρω τ' ἀθανάτω τε
ἔσσεσθ', οὔτε κεν αὐτὸς ἐνὶ πρώτοισι μαχοίμην
οὔτε κε σὲ στέλλοιμι μάχην ἐς κυδιάνειραν·
νῦν δ' (ἔμπης γὰρ κῆρες ἐφεστᾶσιν θανάτοιο
μυρίαι, ἃς οὐκ ἔστι φυγεῖν βροτὸν οὐδ' ὑπαλύξαι)
ἴομεν.

                                                  (*Iliad*, xii. 322-328.)

The particular emphasis with which, according to the narrator, he spoke forth the third line—οὔτε κεν αὐτὸς ἐνὶ πρώτοισι μαχοίμην—was true to a ruling passion which made him the most dangerous of ministers, though no inglorious man.

Carteret was made Secretary of State by the influence of Sunderland, and he took over from his first patron his dislike to the two brother ministers. A strenuous conflict began between the two sections of the government, which ended in 1724 in Carteret's defeat. This has been commonly cited as an instance of Walpole's jealous determination to exclude every superior man from power—a charge on which it is sufficient to remark that Carteret was quite as busy in striving to exclude Walpole and Townshend, as they were in excluding him ; that Townshend had a much more active feeling, and took a more active part than Walpole ; that it was an ordinary case of struggle in a Cabinet, in which, luckily for the country, Carteret happened to have the fortune of war against him ; and, finally, that Walpole would have stultified himself and ruined his whole policy if he had allowed a minister to remain in charge of so momentous a branch of business as foreign affairs, of whom it could be truly said, as Onslow said of Carteret, that " he thought consulting the interior interests and disposition of the people, the conduct of business in Parliaments, and the methods of raising money for the execution even of his own designs, was a work below his applications, and to be left as underparts of government to the care of inferior and subordinate understandings, in subserviency, however, to his will and measures." We need not impute to Walpole an insatiable thirst for power, in order to understand his willingness to part company with a colleague of such temper as this. It is to be observed, further, that Walpole did not hurry to part company with him, for Carteret remained a member of the Cabinet for six years (1724 – 30) after he ceased to be Secretary of State. To be able to work with a man in a Cabinet for ten years, hardly indicates an arrogant aversion to all colleagues of genius.

It was important at this moment to send a strong man to Dublin, for Ireland was shaken by the dangerous agitation which had its origin in Wood's halfpence, but which had its roots much deeper than the mere issue of a patent to an English tradesman to supply a deficiency in Irish coinage. That the issue of the patent was an odious job, by which a large sum of money was to find its way into the pocket of the king's mistress, is undeniable. The amount to be struck was in gross and mischievous excess over what was required, as was shown by the willingness of the government to reduce the sum from more than one hundred thousand pounds to forty thousand. The whole operation was conducted from first to last with a flagrant disregard for Irish opinion or Irish authority, which might be called incredible, if the same principle had not prevailed until now. On the other hand, the unfortunate coins were good and of true value, nor was anybody obliged to take them who did not choose ; and the case against them was marked by many exaggerations, misrepresentations, and lies.

Unluckily for the peace of the British government, the case was taken up by the strongest controversial genius of the age. Swift hated and despised the country in which his unhappy lot was cast, but he had the honest contempt natural to a powerful mind for the wretched system on which it was governed, and he was inspired besides by keen animosity against the party in England and the minister, by whose neglect or ill-will he had been doomed to perpetual exile.

F

The Drapier's Letters are among the very few pieces of political controversy on an ephemeral incident, to which their literary qualities give lasting interest. The fourth of them reveals the real spring of the agitation—the old and ever-renewed protest against the government of Ireland by England. This was one of the too few occasions in Irish history on which the whole nation in both its branches, and of both creeds, spoke with one voice and faced their bad rulers with a united front. It was no feeling of justice, and no interest in good government in Ireland, that prompted the final surrender, but the fear, inspired in the agents of Ascendancy, that the exasperation against Wood and his coins was bringing Catholics and Protestants, Jacobites and Whigs, into an intimacy that was dangerous to the constitutional connection between Great Britain and the sister kingdom. Walpole at once saw the impossibility of forcing the inclinations of a whole people, governed and governors alike. Carteret on the spot—though his own intrigues in Ireland at an earlier stage of the affair will hardly bear examination — now earnestly supported the same view, and, in spite of Townshend and others of their colleagues, the viceroy was authorised to announce to the Irish Parliament that the obnoxious patent was absolutely at an end. Ireland gave Walpole no further trouble. Affairs were mainly guided by the influence of Archbishop Boulter in the English and planter interest; and Walpole appears, when he thought of Ireland at all, to have regarded this as the safest policy.

With the temporary suppression of the Jacobite plots, the subjection of Carteret, the pacification of the ferment in Ireland, the minister found the course of domestic affairs run smoothly enough. Now and at all times it was foreign affairs that demanded most attention; but his policy in this department will be most conveniently viewed in a chapter of its own. The king wished to reward his minister by a peerage. Walpole was the first minister who made the House of Commons the centre of authority, and he declined to leave it. The peerage was conferred upon his eldest son. Among minor expedients for strengthening his influence was one at which philosophers may smile, and which the party leader may in his heart despise, but which for practical purposes he is not likely to overlook. In 1725 Walpole induced the king to revive the Order of the Bath. No creation had been made since 1661. The minister bethought himself of it as a cheap way of rewarding a friend or buying off a possible foe. The bestowal of the red riband, moreover, would be convenient for staving off what is in every generation the importunate demand for the blue. " They who take the Bath," he told the old Duchess of Marlborough, " shall the sooner have the Garter." He set the example by taking the Bath himself, and became Sir Robert. The following year (1726) he resigned this honour, and became a knight of the higher Order.

The fulsome author of the *Night Thoughts* had the previous year received from Walpole a royal pension of two hundred pounds per annum, and he now celebrated the event in his patron's career in some foolish jingle about garter'd sons of praise, our boast of former days, and calling on Britain to see her Walpole shining from afar, his azure Ribbon and his shining Star. It was not a mere poetic figure to call the coveted riband azure; but a few years later it was changed from sky-blue to the modern Garter-blue, in order to distinguish companions of lawful creation from those who had the Order bestowed upon them by the Pretender. Two points excited remark in Walpole's case, and they are worth noticing as signs of the time : one, that he was decorated for merely civil distinction ; the other, that he was a commoner. No commoners had been made Knights of the Garter since Sir Edward Montagu and General Monk in 1660. No commoner after Walpole received the blue riband until Lord North in 1772, and the only other knights of the Order who have sat in the House of Commons since were Castlereagh and Palmerston. Queen Victoria desired to give the Garter to Sir Robert Peel in 1845, but Peel, with a characteristic mixture of shyness and of pride, replied that he sprang from the people and belonged to the people, and that the honour would be inappropriate. We may perhaps wonder that Walpole did not act on the reason afterwards assigned by Lord Melbourne for refusing the Garter ; that he did not see why he should be such a fool as to buy himself, when he could buy somebody else with it. He was possibly guided as usual by motives of policy. " Is ambition imputed to me ? " he asked in his great defence in 1741. " Why, then, do I still continue a commoner —I who refused a white staff and a peerage ? I had, indeed, like to have forgotten the little ornament about my shoulders, which gentlemen have so repeatedly mentioned in terms of sarcastic obloquy. But surely though this may be regarded with envy or indignation in another place, it cannot be supposed to raise any resentment in this House, where many may be pleased to see those honours which their ancestors have worn returned again to the Commons." Sir Bluestring became the favourite nickname, and the composers of mug-house songs for fifteen years to come found their patrons never tired of listening to choruses of which the point was always the same ; that though the knight had laid down the red riband to take up the blue, a third change awaited him yet, when justice would at last be done by the hempen string at Tyburn.

Tyburn was still a long way off, but the elements of an Opposition gradually gathered themselves together. The Tory reaction of Anne was recent, and the state of mind that had made it possible was only quiescent and not extinct. It was Walpole's cue to represent Tory and Jacobite as identical, so as to cover the whole Opposition with the taint of disaffection to the Revolution settlement and the reigning family. This was no mere manœuvre for party purposes. As Hume shows, cavalier and roundhead, court party and country party, Tory and Whig, all represented genuine divisions of principle in our government; neither of them disowned either monarchy or liberty, but men of easy temper, attached to peace and order, would lean towards monarchy, while bolder spirits, passionately devoted to liberty, would value the republican part of our mixed scheme. Abstract principles, however, never bring us to sufficiently close quarters in politics. Principles, as Hume excellently says, are changed into affections. Men are guided by what they take to be the balance between advantages and disadvantages. The chief advantage of the Stuart line was its association with stable and ordered public sentiment : its chief disadvantage was its dissidence from the established religion of the people. The great advantage of the Hanoverian line, on the other hand, was its natural favour for that liberty which had raised it to the throne : its great disadvantage lay in the foreign possessions of the Hanoverian princes, which might involve us in the wars and intrigues of continental Europe.[1]

The practical result of Tory prepossessions is shown by Lord Chancellor Cowper in that remarkable memorial which he laid before George I. on his accession.[2] "Many of the Tories," he says, " would

[1] *Hume's Essays*, i. 133, and 470 (Green's Edition).
[2] This memorial is printed as an appendix to chapter xvii. of Campbell's *Lives of the Chancellors*, but for some reason has been omitted from later editions.

rejoice to see the Pretender restored by a French
power, much more if by any safer means; the
best of them would hazard nothing to keep him
out, though probably do nothing hazardous to
bring him in; but if ever he should declare himself Protestant, with proper circumstances to make
his conversion probable (as, after the death of
the French king and his mother, it is not unlikely
he may do), they would greedily swallow the
cheat, and endeavour by all possible means to
put in practice again their old notions of divine,
hereditary, and indefeasible right, by a restoration
of the person in whom by their opinion that right
is lodged." This remained a true description of
the equivocal and unstable position of the Tories,
for the greater part of Walpole's government. The
least Jacobite among them were still very cold
friends to the new settlement, and for many years
any accident might have turned them into active
enemies. These were the group who followed Sir
William Wyndham—one of the most respectable
figures of his age, notwithstanding the badness of
his cause; a statesman endowed with firmness,
dignity, modesty, and the gift, so hard to define
but so sensible in operation, of imposing his authority upon his hearers.

The Tories, so early as 1728, were joined by
a small group of malcontent Whigs, headed by
William Pulteney, who presently became the leader
of the coalition against Walpole in the Commons,
as Carteret was in the House of Lords. Pulteney
left the main body of the Whigs in disgust at not
receiving either the office or the confidence to which
he justly considered that his talents entitled him.
According to one story, Walpole soon discovered
that he had made a mistake, and immediately
endeavoured to repair it by proposing to make
him Secretary of State, but Pulteney's self-love
had been too deeply wounded. Another version

is that, during the conflict between Townshend and Carteret in 1724, Walpole discovered that Pulteney was intriguing with Carteret, and resolved that as he had chosen to try to gain entrance by that door, the key of the other should be finally turned upon him. Whatever the cause, he went into strong opposition. He was a fine speaker, abounding in sharp epigram and cutting wit, prompt in debate, full of animation and fire, and a master in all the arts of parliamentary attack. But even friendly contemporaries agree that his shining gifts were ruined by uncertainty and instability of mind. "It would be endless," says Chesterfield on one occasion, "to give you an account of the various sallies and extravagances of Pulteney, which change oftener than the wind." Hervey describes him as "vindictive, born with little passions, unequal and uneven, sometimes in very high and sometimes in very low spirits, and full of small enmities." He was so little to be depended on, that the songs represent him as bellowing for liberty to-day, and roaring for power to-morrow, as tight to the Tories at noon, and supping with Whigs at night. He fully deserves Shelburne's remark, that if we examine his long opposition, it will be seen that he never did any good nor attempted to do any. His career was pure faction, and when the hour of triumph arrived, we shall see that he in an instant turned it into the most extraordinary failure in party history.

The secret mover of the machinery of opposition was a wilder and more versatile spirit than any of these, the famous Bolingbroke. We cannot wonder that his own generation should have been dazzled by the genius of a man who had taken the main part in overturning a ministry so covered with glory as that of Marlborough and Godolphin; who showed such unexampled dexterity, alike in framing, carrying, and defending the great instruments of Utrecht ; who led men of such force, brilliancy, and position as Carteret, Pulteney, and Wyndham ; and who finally, as he had contributed more than any one else to the fall of Marlborough, now boldly applied himself to sap the power of the minister who was as strong and as successful in civil government as Marlborough had ever been in the field.[1] The misanthropy of Swift, the mockery of Voltaire, the sensitiveness of Pope, were all overcome by the fascination of his address, the glitter of his ideas, and the eloquence of his talk, Swift wrote to Stella that Mr. St. John was the greatest young man he ever knew—wit, capacity, beauty, quickness of apprehension, good learning, and excellent taste ; the best orator in the House of Commons, admirable conversation, good nature, and good manners ; generous and a despiser of money.[2] Another of his friends vowed, in a grand transport of praise, that the writings and conversation of Bolingbroke did nothing less than unite the wisdom of Socrates, the dignity and ease of Pliny, and the wit of Horace. In every part he was a consummate posture-master—the stoical philosopher musing on the true uses of retirement and study, the statesman busily framing policies, erecting combinations, and moulding foolish princes into patriot kings, or the simple country gentleman smoking tobacco with his honest neighbours, inquiring how the wheat was doing in the four-acre field, and careful to know the names of all his hounds. Parallels to this extraordinary man have been sought all through history, from Alcibiades down to Lord Byron ; he supplied the best poet of his day with philosophy ; made speeches that intoxicated the House of Commons, and left such a tradition that illustrious authorities declared that

[1] See Walpole's *George II.* i. 222.
[2] 1st November 1711.

they would rather recover one of Bolingbroke's
orations than the lost books of Livy, or " all the
gaps in Greek and Roman lore " ; he developed
ideas on statecraft and the constitution which have
lived to find some favour among eminent men
even in our own time ; and finally, he handled the
great and difficult instrument of written language
with such freedom and copiousness, such vivacity
and ease, that in spite of much literary foppery
and falsetto he ranks, in all that musicians call
execution, only below the three or four highest
masters of English prose. Yet of all the char-
acters in our history, Bolingbroke must be pronounced to be most of a charlatan ; of all the
writing in our literature, his is the hollowest, the
flashiest, the most insincere.

Impeached in England he fled to France,
entered the service of the Pretender, and within
a year, just as he was being attainted for high
treason at Westminster, he was at the same time
impeached for treason by his new master at St.
Germains. After this unique experience he re-
freshed himself by a draught of what he called
consolatio philosophica, and composed *Reflections
upon Exile,* an edifying collection of platitudes
freely borrowed from Seneca. His sense of the
beauties of exile did not prevent him from abject
efforts to bring it to an end. No bankrupt
politician ever surpassed his dissimulation. He
hastened to pay court to Walpole's brother in
Paris, entered into correspondence with the English
ministers to the detriment of his old Jacobite
friends, at the same time intrigued against the
English ministers with the French government,
and finally, after finding out Carteret's intrigues
with the Tories, carried their secrets over to the
Whigs. A much more effective step was to bribe
the Duchess of Kendal with a present of eleven
thousand pounds, as the price of his restoration.

Walpole was given to understand that if he did not comply he would be dismissed, and as a compromise he passed a bill for the restitution of the family estates, but maintaining the exclusion from Parliament. In his own day, Walpole was always blamed by his friends for mistaken lenity in consenting to Bolingbroke's return. According to the temper of modern times, we are more disposed to think him weak for not making the amnesty complete. Bolingbroke's restless ambition, his inveterate love of plots and schemes, his passion for display, were sure to make him the minister's enemy, and his enmity could not have been more injurious in the comparative privacy of the House of Lords, than it proved to be in the pages of the *Craftsman.* As it was, his vigour, hardihood, and resource made him for ten years the intellectual inspirer of the Opposition both in the press and in Parliament. He had been a Tory highflier, he had been a whimsical, he had been James's Secretary of State ; he now became a Whig of the Whigs, denounced legitimacy and legitimists, and, not content modestly to savour the graces of conversion, he insisted on figuring as the only orthodox interpreter of Revolution principles, and with righteous anger branded Walpole for endangering the untold blessings of the Revolution settlement. Ingenuity was never carried farther than in Bolingbroke's efforts to invent phrases that should catch the followers of Wyndham without startling the friends of Pulteney, and should persuade both that they were engaged in " a virtuous defence of the constitution." Bolingbroke was not without the daemonic elements of character : he had fire, energy, penetration, insight, elasticity, fertility, imagination, adventure. But neither his character nor the flimsy and incongruous creations of his political fancy were calculated to attract the country gentlemen. They keenly relished his attacks on the minister. They sometimes took his hints about motions and divisions and the mystery of electioneering; but they cared very little about the ideal of a Patriot King, and had not the least intention of allowing Prerogative to become the substitute for Influence. They used his talents, but he was never either trusted or popular. Wyndham alone seems to have been warmly and sincerely his friend. The staunch Jacobites hated him as having betrayed their master. The honest Whigs hated him as a Tory renegado. Even the malcontent Whigs suspected and disliked him. They knew in their hearts that there was no answer possible to Walpole's scathing description of him, in one of his most apt and energetic passages, as ferreting out information for the benefit of foreign ambassadors, as making it his trade to betray the secrets of every court as soon as he left it, as betraying every master he ever served, as void of all faith and all honour.[1] In the face of perfidies like these, it is hardly worth while to dwell on mere inconsistencies in policy : to note that he who had made peace with France the keystone of his system, now assailed Walpole for not being German ; that the minister of Queen Anne who originated the newspaper stamp, was the loudest champion of the absolute freedom of the press ; or that the proposer of the first commercial treaty proved the fiercest opponent of Walpole's move towards free trade. As might have been expected, he resorted to a common device of embarrassed politicians ; he called for a national party. The hypocritical phrase did not make his allies forget that it was he who had first insisted on drawing strict party lines and driving the Whigs out of government, any more than it prevented the revival, when power was once more within reach, of the acutest jealousies between the

[1] Coxe, ch. xlii., iii. 148.

two wings of the patriot coalition. "When I
was young," Burke says, "a general fashion told
me I was to admire some of the writings against
Sir Robert Walpole ; a little more maturity taught
me as much to despise them." Chatham confessed
to the same contempt, though Bolingbroke had
been his friend and political coadjutor. The verdict
has been confirmed by the judgment of posterity.
In vain the consummate artist strives to disguise
the shipwrecked adventurer. In vain does he
borrow the graces and polish of Plato or Cicero,
to turn pamphleteering into philosophy. The
flowing rhythm, the impetuosity, the affected union
of a student's gravity with the gay breeding of a
man of the world, may please the idle ear, but
neither in fact nor observation, nor in his own
conviction, have his writings foundation or bottom.[1]
It seems to be very doubtful whether, even in
his own day, either Bolingbroke's writings or his
machinations ever did Walpole real damage. It
must not be forgotten that after he had been ten
years incessantly at work Bolingbroke went back
to France (1735), according to some, because
Walpole had found him out in treasonable intrigues
with a foreign minister ; according to others, because Pulteney plainly told him that " his name
and presence in England did hurt." Whatever the
reason of his retreat, he went in the mood of a
baulked gambler, bitterly disgusted with his confederates, and professing much virtuous surprise
at the painful discovery that what they had been
aiming at all the time was not the reform of government, but the succession to Walpole ; not a virtuous
defence of the constitution, as he had in his inno-
cence been dreaming, but " a dirty intrigue of low
ambition."

---

[1] Bolingbroke has been made the subject of several interesting criti-
cisms, of which the brilliant essay of Churton Collins and a masterly study
by Robert Harrop are the most important.

There was a moment when Walpole seems to have apprehended serious danger from Bolingbroke. The same influences that had forced the minister to assent to his return, were actively at work to procure his admission to power. The matter is very obscure, and perhaps is now hardly worth unravelling, even if it were possible. The authority of the mistress over the king, and the weight of Bolingbroke's bribes with the mistress, were certainly thought by Walpole to constitute a standing peril, and the fluctuations of Hanoverian policy and interest undoubtedly opened a field admirably suited to Bolingbroke's genius for intrigue. He took the bold step of insisting that the king should give his enemy an audience and hear all that he had to say. As might have been expected, mercurial plausibilities were little calculated to move the saturnine mind of the king. " *Bagatelles, bagatelles,*" he answered, when Walpole asked him what Bolingbroke had said. Bolingbroke resembled De Retz in genius for intrigue, though far inferior to him in intrepidity and courage, and so now, just as De Retz, when he found himself repulsed at court, directed all his passion and his hate against Mazarin, Bolingbroke made the destruction of Walpole the object of his life, to be effected by calumny, by wit, by invective and ridicule, by every appeal to the selfishness of bad men and the unguarded prepossessions of the good.

CHAPTER V

An event now occurred which was by many confidently expected to bring Walpole's career as minister to an end. In the summer of 1727 George I. died on the road to Hanover. The news found Walpole in his rural villa at Chelsea. He instantly rode off to Richmond as fast as he could, to announce to the new king what had happened. The. prince always retired to rest after his midday dinner, and there Walpole found him. For some time he disbelieved the news, and refused to get out of bed to be told that he was king, as stubbornly as Barnardine in the play refuses Abhorson's summons to rise and be hanged. When he was at length convinced that his father was dead, he dismissed the minister with a curt command to seek Sir Spencer Compton at Chiswick, and from him to take his directions. This was what Walpole had expected. His fidelity to the interests of his former master had apparently ensured the enmity of his successor. As the son hated his father, he could not well love his father's most trusted adviser.

Compton was a younger son of the family of Northampton, and had been Speaker in three Parliaments. In this capacity he had been successful and popular, and had shown some resource. When a member desired that order might be kept, for he had a right to be heard, the Speaker would make the ingenious rejoinder, " No, sir, you have a right to speak, but the House have a right to judge whether they will hear you." Besides being Speaker, he had been the prince's treasurer ever since his arrival in England. His selection to be the new minister would therefore have been natural ; but the old men were not displaced at once, and before many days were over the king made up his mind not to displace them at all. At the time of the accommodation between the old king and his son, seven years before, Walpole seems to have had as much influence with the Princess of Wales as he ever acquired over her as queen,[1] and the new circumstances may well have revived old impressions.

At first, things at the new court underwent the change of face in which satirists of every age and tongue rejoice. Leicester House, in the old king's lifetime, had been shunned like a city stricken with the plague ; all at once it became thronged from morning to night. Walpole, whose steps had so long been dogged by a mob of toadies and place-hunters, now made vacancy wherever he turned. Compton held levees, crowded by men who had sworn in prose and verse that no adverse fate should ever separate them from Sir Robert. The new king's feelings towards the three principal · men in his father's government had never been concealed. Walpole he was accustomed freely to describe as rogue and rascal ; the Duke of Newcastle was an impertinent fool ; and Townshend a choleric blockhead. Yet the experience of a few days was enough to show the king that the rascal, the impertinent, and the blockhead were the three best servants that he was likely to find. Compton's incompetency was manifest within four-and-twenty hours. He had, moreover, committed the indiscretion of making the new king's wife his enemy by paying court to the mistress, and he was the

[1] Lady Cowper's *Diary*, under date 1720.

first to find that the enmity of the new queen was invariably fatal to its object. But still more important causes worked for the retention of the old ministry.

The most formidable danger to be apprehended, alike for English and for Hanoverian interests, was any change in the friendly attitude of France. Happily Cardinal Fleury saw no reason why the substitution of George II. for George I. should affect the interests or policy of France. He explained his views to Horace Walpole, the British ambassador : France would hold firm to all her engagements as one of the allies of Hanover, if the new king would adhere to the system of his father, and to the old principle that the common security of the two countries lay in steadfast union. Fleury, moreover, sensibly assuring the ambassador that more would be done in a couple of days of conversation than by volumes of despatches, urged him to repair at once to London and lay his views before the king. When Walpole arrived, the king began by scolding him after his usual manner for quitting his post without leave. Then, when the preliminary blustering was over and the cardinal's letter was produced, King George was too acute not to see what good news the ambassador had brought, and at the same time how much easier it would be to steer the same course if the same ministers remained at the helm.

The delicate operation of fixing the amount of the civil list turned equally in Walpole's favour. The Whigs out of place, regarding office as the object of a party auction, strove to outbid the Whigs in place. Now this was a sort of play at which Walpole was not easy to beat. Compton proposed that the queen's jointure should be settled at £60,000 ; Walpole offered to ask Parliament for £100,000. The grant to the late king had been £700,000 a year. Walpole gave it to be understood

that he would put it at £800,000, and at this sum
it was finally settled. The king, in the conversation
with Walpole in which these terms were discussed,
took him by the hand and said, " Consider, Sir
Robert, what makes me easy in this matter will
prove for your ease too ; it is for my life it is to
be fixed, and it is for your life."

Before the courtiers could guess what was
going on, Compton had, with tears in his eyes,
declared his incapacity for so arduous a trust,
and Walpole and Townshend were once more re-
installed. As Walpole drove through St. James's
Square, he saw Sir Spencer Compton's house
besieged by people of all ranks eager to worship
the rising sun. " Did you observe," he said to a
friend, "how my house is deserted, and how that
door is crowded with carriages ? To-morrow this
house will be deserted, and mine will be more
frequented than ever." Before the secret was out,
his wife went to pay her respects at Leicester
House. She could not, says her son, make her
way between the scornful backs and sharp elbows
of the fine people who had a few days before been
her steadfast devotees. When the queen called out,
" I think I see a friend," and beckoned her forward,
everybody eagerly made way ; " and as I came
back," said Lady Walpole, " I might have walked
over their heads if I pleased." It is not surprising
that Walpole failed to take exalted views of human
nature ; at least he had good sense and breadth of
mind enough to keep clear of a cheap and shallow
misanthropy.

The remarkable woman who now made her first
appearance on the stage of great affairs was to
play an important part in Walpole's career. Caroline of Anspach came of a branch of the house of
Brandenburg. Having lost her father early, the
young princess was partially brought up in Berlin.
There, in the society of Sophia Charlotte — the

G

friend of Leibnitz and so inquisitively curious that, as Leibnitz said of her, she would know even the why of a why — she acquired that keenness of mind for speculative subjects, and that respect for learning and learned men, which distinguished her from the rest of the gross and unlettered representatives of the Hanoverian stock in England. She possessed by nature the same cheerful, brisk, curious, acute, and stirring character, as both the queen, Sophia Charlotte, and her mother, the old Electress Sophia. She sometimes recalls, too, Charlotte Elizabeth of Bavaria, the niece of the Electress Sophia and cousin therefore of George II., who married the brother of Louis XIV., became the mother of the Regent Orleans, and watched for so many years with shrewd, honest, amazed eyes the strange distractions and devilries of her vile husband and her corrupted son. Queen Caroline's life, like the lives of these her kinswomen so oddly mated, can hardly have been a very happy one, if happiness means the regular satisfaction of our best aims and highest faculties ; but she had that reasonable substitute for happiness which lies in cheerful stoicism, in an active constancy of mind, and in a clear-eyed resolution to see men and things as they are.

George II. was always called by his cousin, Frederick William, the terrible father of Frederick the Great, " My brother the comedian." He had the strut, the gesticulation, the bustle of the bad play-actor, and, like the bad actor, he was all the more eager for applause, because he inwardly suspected that he only half deserved it. He was not without sterling qualities. He had physical courage : in Marlborough's wars he had served with credit ; and even his father, who hated him, admitted that he fought like a man. He knew how to keep a secret, and he was proud of being a man of honour and a man of his word. This did not

prevent him from snatching his father's will from
the hands of the Archbishop of Canterbury at his
first Council, walking out of the room with the
will in his pocket, and taking care that it should
never be heard of again. He treated the will of his
uncle, the Duke of York, with equally little ceremony. The shade of George I. could not have
complained, for he had burnt both his wife's will
and her father's. Yet George II. was rather above
than below the standard of veracity current in his
time. When Hervey observed to Walpole that
the king would not lie, " Not often," Walpole
replied. He was sober and temperate in most of
his appetites, though not in all; and his habits
were methodical to a point of mechanical regularity
that drove those who had to live with him almost
mad. His drives in the afternoon, his commerce
and backgammon at night, his levees and audiences
in the morning, were all fixed to the instant, so
that, as the weary courtiers complained, with an
almanack for the day of the week, and a watch
for the hour of the day, everybody would know
precisely what point in the mill-horse track the
court was passing. It was his habit to visit the
favourite, Mrs. Howard, every evening in her own
apartments at nine o'clock, with such mechanical
punctuality that he often walked about his chamber
for ten minutes with his watch in his hand, waiting
for the blissful moment. A mistake by a valet
would throw him into such agitation, that people
who came into the room supposed that he must
have just received some dreadful piece of news.
In ordinary intercourse he was stiff, formal, and
uneasy, as men are apt to be who privately doubt
their own fitness for a post, but hope that their
secret is not found out. He had a laudable impatience with people who did not come quickly
to the point; and one of the many reasons why
he hated the admission of Pitt to office, was that

the great commoner treated him to grand speeches in the closet ; they might, he said, be uncommonly fine, but were quite beyond his comprehension. The king's confidence was hard to gain, and he was reserved in showing it, but he was never unstable : he steadily respected the judgment of the queen ; he was firm as a rock for Walpole ; and when the time came, he fought like a lion for Carteret. With all his faults, we must give such a man credit for character. He was avaricious and mean. The only personal gift that he ever made to Walpole was a diamond, and it was found to be cracked through. His temper was passionate and splenetic, and he was an incessant railer. Though not exactly bad-hearted or malevolent, he was thoroughly unfeeling. He is described as timorous in Council. " He thinks he is devilish stout," said Walpole once, when the king was bent on going to Hanover, and the minister was resolved that he should not, " and that he never gives up his will or his opinion, but he never acts in anything material but when I have a mind that he should. Our master, like most people's masters, wishes himself absolute, and fancies he has courage enough to attempt making himself so ; but if I know anything of him, he is, with all his personal bravery, as great a political coward as ever wore a crown."

This was the man whom it was the great business of the queen's life to humour, to cajole, to amuse, to restrain, and to lead. She acquired complete ascendancy over him, but it was purchased at a merciless price, and it needed to be carefully hidden. In spite of his self-satisfaction the king was too sharp not to know that every design, project, and combination which he found in his mind, had been laboriously planted there by concert between Walpole and the queen. But he flattered himself that nobody else knew it. To make the comedy perfect, he was never weary of gibing at sovereigns who had been governed by women and by favourites. Charles I. was ruled by his wife, Charles II. by his mistresses, James II. by his priests, King William by his Dutchmen, Queen Anne by Lady Marlborough and Lady Masham. He wound up his list with a smile of triumph by asking, " And who do they say governs now ? "

The king had, almost to the end, not only a great admiration for the queen's judgment, but also, in spite of his unfaithfulness, a strong attachment to her person. When he was absent in Hanover, he wrote letters to the queen thirty pages long, as warm and tender as those of " a young sailor of twenty to his first mistress." This did not prevent him from being rough and uncivil, even when he meant to be kind. One half of his conversation with her was made up of what its unfortunate victim called snappings and snubbings ; and he was in all circumstances intolerably exacting. He hated the company of men as much as he delighted in that of women ; and as he could not bear to be alone, the queen was obliged, for many hours in every day, to watch him strutting and fuming about her apartment, to listen to his rude and irascible tirades with affected interest, to return insults with obsequious flattery, and to practise all the other slavish artifices by which unlucky women of sense are so often compelled to manage their tyrants. His Majesty comes into the gallery, snubs the queen, who happens to be drinking chocolate, for always stuffing ; one princess for not hearing him, and another for being grown fat ; one of his sons for standing awkwardly ; Lord Hervey for not knowing what relation the Prince of Sulzbach was to the Elector Palatine ; and then he carries off the queen to receive more snubs in the garden. The queen ventures to make some remark to Hervey about Bishop Hoadley's book on the sacraments. The king, breaking in, asks her why she loves talking such nonsense about things she knows nothing about, as if it were not fools loving to talk of such things that made the fools who wrote upon them publish their nonsense. Then he turns to Hervey and tells him that if the Bishop of Winchester is his friend, he has a great puppy and a very dull fellow and a great rascal for his friend. " It is a very pretty thing for such scoundrels, when they are raised by favour so much above their desert, to be talking and writing their stuff, to give trouble to the government that has showed them that favour ; and very modest in a canting hypocritical knave to be crying, ' The kingdom of Christ is not of this world,' at the same time that he as Christ's ambassador receives six thousand a year." So the torrent of petulance every day ran on for hour after hour, the queen all the time, by smiles and nods at the right places, endeavouring to signify her approval of his wisdom, to keep herself as safely out of mischief as she could, and to prevent onlookers from discerning the depth of her humiliation and chagrin. For an hour or two before bedtime he would talk about armies or about genealogies, whilst the queen knitted and yawned. " She was at least seven or eight hours *tête-à-tête* with the king every day, during which time she was generally saying what she did not think, assenting to what she did not believe, and praising what she did not approve. She used to give him her opinion as jugglers do a card, by changing it imperceptibly, and making him believe he held the same as that he first pitched upon. But that which made these *tête-à-têtes* seem heaviest was that he neither liked reading nor being read to (unless it was to sleep) ; she was forced like a spider to spin out of her own bowels all the conversation with which the fly was taken. For all the tedious hours she spent in watching him

while he slept, or the heavier task of entertaining
him while he was awake, her single consolation
was in reflecting she had power, and that people
in coffee - houses were saying she governed their
country, without knowing how dear the government of it cost her" (Hervey). We may judge
how deadly the weariness became from the story
that when Lady Suffolk was falling out of favour,
the Princess Royal actually said that she wished
with all her heart that her father would take
somebody else, "that mamma might be a little
relieved from the *ennui* of seeing him for ever in
her room."

No private complaisance was thought by the
queen too hard to be borne, so long as it helped
her to retain exclusive access to the king's ear in
public affairs. No humiliation was too abject, if she
could only restrain his variable impulses, and guide
him along the path that was indicated by her good
Sir Robert. Walpole often told her that she was
the sole mover of the court, and that if he could
boast of any success in carrying on the king's
affairs, it was all due to her mediation. "For if,"
he said, "I have had the merit of giving any good
advice to the king, all the merit of making him
take it, madam, is entirely your own, and so much
so, that I not only never did do anything without
you, but I know I never could." When courtiers
heard the queen using metaphors about not hanging
every hound that ran a little slower than the rest,
provided in the main it kept up with the pack,
they knew very well, and even the king must have
guessed, that the imagery came from Norfolk and
not from Hanover.

Though the king and queen were from their
position the useful guardians of our free constitution, they had no predilection for political liberty.
The dapper martinet is said always to have hated
his English subjects as republicans and killers of

kings. Even the queen, filled as she was by the stiff and narrow ideas of German courts, was never cordially reconciled to the dependence in which the king was held upon ministers and Parliament. In her heart it was odious to her that the king should be the pensioner of his people, forced to go to the House of Commons for every shilling that he needed. Though she was ready to dispense with ceremony when it stood in the way of her convenience, as when she conversed with Lord Hervey for two hours through the half-open door of her bedroom, she always held high notions of regal etiquette. She sometimes honoured Sir Robert by dining at his house in Chelsea. The queen, we are told, sat down to table with Lady Walpole and any member of the royal family whom she had brought with her. Sir Robert stood behind her chair, handed her the first dish, and then retired into another room, where he dined with the queen's household attendants. On the other hand, Walpole and the queen were on terms of familiarity in their discourse which would now be not only amazing between any royal consort and a minister, but between any decent man and any decent woman. It is painful, even at this distance of time, when they have all shrunk into thin ghosts and shadows of names, to read some of the jests with which Walpole regaled the queen, at her own expense and to her profound secret discomfiture as a woman.

Much as the queen had to endure in her masculine desire for power, her use of it was uniformly for good. She had a thorough grasp of the principles of Walpole's policy, she comprehended and sympathised with his temper and his maxims, and she perceived as clearly as Walpole himself how closely the stability of the dynasty was bound up with the firm maintenance of a parliamentary constitution. No two personages were ever more fitted thoroughly

to understand one another than Walpole and
Queen Caroline. The queen, however, had some
higher intellectual interests, which to Walpole
probably seemed as pure nonsense as they seemed
to King George. She often tried to make him
read Butler's *Analogy*, but he told her that his
religion was fixed, and that he had no desire either
to change or to improve it. " At no period in the
history of our Church," says a good authority,
" has the ecclesiastical patronage of the Crown
been better directed than while it was secretly
dispensed by Queen Caroline ; for a brief period
liberality and cultivation of mind were passports
to promotion in the Church." [1] She offered a
bishopric to Berkeley, and her recommendation
led to the preferment of Butler to Durham.
Hoadley was too political and too liberal in his
politics to be a favourite with crowned heads, but
Hare and Sherlock were among her best friends.
Her own theological views undoubtedly leaned to
the latitudinarian, the tolerant, and the heterodox,
and were presumably as empty of spiritual force
as the rest of the rationalism of the time. In her
girlhood a marriage had been projected with the
archduke who afterwards became the Emperor
Charles VI., and she had with that design been
instructed in the great controversies between the
two creeds, with a view to her conversion to the
Romish Church. When the marriage was abandoned, it was found that instead of preferring
either faith to the other, she had learned to suspect both. Her favourite divine was Dr. Samuel
Clarke. With him once a week, in the midst of
courtiers and fine ladies, she discussed whether
the will is free, whether the annihilation of time
and space is beyond the power of Omnipotence
itself, whether the First Person of the Holy Trinity
can annihilate the Second and the Third. Clarke

[1] Pattison, *Essays*, ii. 109.

once went with Sir Isaac Newton, to help the great philosopher to explain to her his immortal system. The queen wished to make Clarke a bishop, and employed Walpole to overcome the good man's scruples. The incongruous pair fought the question until the candles were burnt down to the socket; but Walpole found that a metaphysician is not so easily persuaded for his own good as a member of Parliament. According to another story, the queen thought of making Clarke Archbishop of Canterbury, until she was told that he was indeed the most learned and most honest man in the king's dominions, and only in one respect unfit for the see, namely, that he was not a Christian. What is at least as interesting as the queen's correspondence with Leibnitz, or her discrimination in the selection of superior divines,—she was the steady patron of Handel. Even the tranquil atmosphere of art was invaded by the passions of political party, and the court was for Handel because the Prince of Wales was for Bononcini. Handel's noblest work was not produced until after Queen Caroline's death, but she deserves credit for her early recognition of the one resplendent genius who soars above the prosaic level of that uninspired and uninspiring time.

No apology is needed for dwelling at length on the personal character and conduct of the king and queen. To-day the immediate source of a minister's strength is the favour of the House of Commons. In the first half of the eighteenth century the immediate source of strength was the favour of the court. The king was at the mercy of the Whig clans—the Pelhams, the Cavendishes, the Cobhams; but among their representatives he was often able to exercise a limited choice for the first place. He could choose whether the head of the administration should be Sunderland, or Townshend, or Walpole, or Carteret, or Pelham.

To this extent the government was the personal
government of the king; and the wearisome intrigues that preceded the installation of Walpole,
that were always ready to spring up during his
supremacy, and that broke out into dire activity
immediately after his fall, were the natural results
of the king's position as limited arbiter in the
personal wrangles of the oligarchy.

Walpole enjoyed the favour of the court because
he was able by prudent and skilful management of
the House of Commons to obtain supplies, and it
was one of his prime maxims both to keep on good
terms with the popular House and to exalt its
place in the constitution. But it is a great mistake to suppose that Walpole was ever a popular
minister. Dr. Johnson once drew a striking and
a sound distinction between Walpole's position
and that of the first Pitt. Walpole, he said, was a
minister given by the king to the people; Pitt was
a minister given by the people to the king. This
was true and significant. Never at any time did
Walpole approach the popularity of the elder Pitt
in 1757, of the younger Pitt in 1784, or of Canning
in 1827. The same remark has been made of Sir
Robert Peel, that not even when he reached the
summit of power in 1841 did his fame shine out
like that of these three illustrious predecessors.
Peel established his power on the confidence of
the middle classes, and Walpole undoubtedly in
the same way was trusted by the monied interests
of his day. But the trust placed in him by the
monied interests, and his gradual reconciliation
with the landed interest, would have been of no
avail without the steady favour of the court.

As it is a mistake to suppose that Walpole ever
rode on the flood tide of popularity in its modern
sense, so is it a mistake to regard his ascendancy as having been undisputed from the fall of
Sunderland. He had loyally shared power with his

principal colleague, and it was not until some time after the accession of George II. that his supremacy became absolute. Walpole's favour with the queen hastened the rupture between the minister and Lord Townshend. For thirty years they had been intimate friends, and for twenty years out of the thirty they had been close political confederates. They were both strict and constant Whigs. They both suffered the censure of the Tory Parliament of Queen Anne. They acted together in the first administration of George I., and they left it together at the schism from the Sunderland Whigs in 1717. They both rejoined their old colleagues in 1720, and both resumed their old posts in 1721 ; they expected a common disgrace on the accession of George II., and had instead been maintained in their offices as the two pillars of a common policy. All this time Townshend had held the more prominent situation of the two. The Secretary of State was higher in the official ordering than any other political minister. Townshend was a noble, was much the greatest man in his county, and had far the finest house. Walpole was a commoner, had only moderate means, and was for long no higher in station than a score of other Norfolk gentlemen. All this had changed. Walpole had slowly risen by sheer weight of character and ability to be by far the foremost man in the House of Commons. By means of which I shall have something to say later, he had acquired money or credit enough to build himself one of the greatest mansions, not only in Norfolk, but in all England. He had made his eldest son a peer, secured a provision for every member of his family, and decorated himself with a badge that was coveted by kings and princes. The friendship of Queen Caroline now gave him the same pre-eminence in the counsels of the king, as Townshend had in the previous reign enjoyed by his favour with the Duchess of

Kendal. This inversion of parts was more than Townshend could bear. His conduct after his fall shows him to have been a really honourable and high-minded man, in times when honour and magnanimity were rare among public personages. But he was proud, impetuous, self-confident, very impatient of criticism or contradiction, not persuasive nor lucid in explaining himself, and therefore often heated and passionate, as those who are not lucid are apt to be. He could not endure banter, and Walpole sometimes bantered him even in the royal presence. Finally it was bitter to him to see the decorous hospitalities of Rainham eclipsed by the roystering of Houghton.

Apart from these grounds of personal grudge, the two ministers began to differ in serious things. Walpole had hitherto contented himself with a general hand in foreign politics. When Townshend made the Treaty of Hanover, Walpole disapproved of a measure for which he would have to find money, and which he would have against his better judgment to defend in a House of Commons where it was extremely unpopular. He openly expressed these views, and gave it to be understood that the man who had to devise the means, and to persuade the House to pass the measure, must have a dominant voice in the policy. With characteristic wisdom he distrusted elaborate schemes of foreign policy, and hated all complicated engagements; Townshend, on the contrary, delighted in them, and the more complicated and entangling they were, the more consummate he thought them.

"As long as the firm was Townshend and Walpole," said Sir Robert in a well-known sentence, "the utmost harmony prevailed; but it no sooner became Walpole and Townshend than things went wrong." Friendship declined into coolness, and coolness grew to open estrangement. One evening at Windsor the queen asked the pair where they had dined. Walpole said that Townshend had dined with a certain elderly lady of quality, of remarkable ugliness, upon whose virtue he could not but think that his lordship had designs. Townshend took fire at the jest, and with a voice shaking with passion, cried out to Walpole, whose own licence was notorious and unblushing, " I have not either a constitution that requires such practices, a purse that can support them, or a conscience that can digest them." Walpole good-naturedly tried to turn the matter aside, but it needed all the queen's tact to pacify his angry colleague. On another occasion at this time, a much more violent altercation took place ; the two great men seized one another by the collar in a lady's drawing-room, grasped the hilts of their swords, and were with much difficulty parted, amid their hostess's shrill screams for the guard. In 1729 Townshend, discerning that his position was thoroughly secondary, gave in his resignation, and retired with dignity and composure into private life. He never returned to public affairs. Chesterfield once went to beg him to come up to the House of Lords, to oppose ministers on some important business. Townshend replied that he knew he was extremely warm, his temper and his personal feelings might hurry him into things which in his cooler moments he should be sorry for, and that he was irrevocably determined to have no more to do with public affairs. We can only wonder at the strange fascination of politics, which has made such honourable self-command as Townshend's so uncommon among statesmen whose ambition has missed its mark.

CHAPTER VI

CHARACTERISTICS

RULERS who have gained historic fame by war and empire, naturally impose heroic and commanding traits on mankind : rulers who have been great in peace usually move us by the qualities of a wise and benign morality. Sir Robert Walpole's position is in this respect a peculiar one. He was a powerful ruler, who guided the country through a long and profoundly critical ordeal ; yet his name possesses no heroic associations. He was a great peace minister, yet his career suggests neither the attractions of private virtue nor the inspiration of lofty public ideals. It is impossible to make one of the grand heroic figures of human history out of nothing more sublime than strong sagacity, penetrating common sense, and tenacious public spirit. Both the nature of Walpole's task and the characteristics of his time were fatal to the heroic. *Quieta non movere* was a sound and saving maxim for a British minister from the Peace of Utrecht to the Seven Years' War ; but it is a maxim without lustre. Although, however, there is nothing in such a character as Walpole's to dazzle or to inspire, he possessed in the highest degree, and displayed on the widest scale, those qualities of intelligence, prudence, watchfulness, and unshaken constancy, which fit a man to act a great part in the trying field of civil contention.

The portraits convey no striking impression of

character. The glance is firm, but the ruling trait
is a somewhat unattractive complacency. Songs
and caricatures abound in references to an ever-
lasting expression between a smile and a sneer.
" His face was bronzed over with a glare of confidence," says his enemy in the *Craftsman*, " an arch
malignity leered in his eye." The malignity is
certainly not there, but the confidence is. In his
early days handsome and portly, he grew afterwards to be corpulent and unwieldy, though he rode
to hounds almost to the last.

He was the gayest and easiest of companions.
Pope was the intimate of Bolingbroke, Swift, and
others of Walpole's bitterest foes, and yet he paid
to the enemy of his friends the tribute of those
graceful lines—

> Seen him I have ; but in his happier hour
> Of social pleasure ill-exchanged for power ;
> Seen him uncumbered with the venal tribe,
> Smile without art and win without a bribe.

" It would have done you good," his son said,
" to hear him laugh." As another said of him, in
an admirable phrase, " he laughed the heart's
laugh." Speaker Onslow said that his goodness
of heart made him the best man to live with, and
to live under, that he ever knew. Pulteney, who
had been his friend and quarrelled with him, and
therefore was inclined to say particularly hard
things of him, declared that Walpole was of a
temper so calm and equal, and so hard to be
provoked, that he never felt the bitterest invectives
against him for half an hour. Of Pelham, his pupil
and successor, it was said that until he lost his
temper he could never exert his reason. Walpole
was the very opposite. He once lost his temper
at a Cabinet, but he immediately broke up the
meeting, remarking that nobody was fit for business
with a ruffled temper. Even Johnson, who thought
that the first Whig was the devil, and who always

took care in reporting the parliamentary debates that the Whig dogs should have the worst of it, still admired Walpole for his placability, and admitted that he was a fine fellow.

A contemporary story gives a singular glimpse of the easy terms on which Walpole stood with men who every day denounced him as the vilest of wretches. Pulteney, though he had seceded from the regulars of his party, supposed, childishly enough, that the virtue of Whig principles would remain in him if he continued to sit on Whig benches. One day,

" Mr. Pulteney, sitting upon the same bench with Sir Robert Walpole in the House of Commons, said : ' Sir Robert, I have a favour to ask of you.' ' O, my good friend Pulteney,' said Sir Robert, ' what favour can you have to ask of me ? ' ' It is,' said Mr. Pulteney, ' that Dr. Pearce may not suffer in his preferment for being my friend.' ' I promise you,' returned Sir Robert, ' that he shall not.' ' Why, then, I hope,' said Mr. Pulteney, ' that you will give him the deanery of Wells.' ' No,' replied Sir Robert, ' I cannot promise you that for him, for it is already promised.' " [1]

Walpole gave Pulteney's friend another deanery, and Pulteney, thinking gratitude for private favours a higher virtue than regard for the public weal, wrote to the new dean to vote for Sir Robert's man if there should be a contest at Winchester. The bonhomie of the House of Commons is very super-ficial, and there was nothing to prevent Pulteney, after writing to his dean, from fulminating against the enormities of Walpole in buying votes by con-ferring places.

Like his father before him, Walpole was a lover of company. There are few more curious pictures of conviviality under difficulties than that of George I., after a morning's hunting at Richmond, drinking

punch and talking dog Latin with Walpole all the
afternoon. The minister was not a drunkard, as
Harley, Carteret, and Daniel Pulteney all were.
Though he probably consumed a quantity that in
modern opinion would constitute a hard drinker,
he was too laborious and systematic a worker all
his life to have been habitually addicted to gross
excess. The vast augmentation of public business
since his day, due to extension of dominion, to
immense increase of population, to rapidity and
multiplicity of communications, to the vigilance of
the newspapers, and to the boundless activity and
exactingness of a reformed House of Commons,
has doubtless made a great difference in the weight
of ministerial burdens. Still there will always be
industrious ministers and lazy ministers, whether
the work of the department be heavy or light ; and
Walpole was one of the most industrious ministers
that ever sat in Downing Street.[1] Some of his
industry was such as few men of business would
now regard as sensible. According to Coxe, he
seldom employed a secretary. Every letter of his
that has been found was wholly written in his
own hand ; and it is believed that the copies in
the Hardwicke collection were taken from originals
all in his own writing. He even underwent the
slavery of transcribing whole letters from other
people, and we are assured that the family papers
abounded with extracts from despatches, and
memoranda upon them, which prove his indefatigable exertions. He always thought for himself, and never fell into the too common weakness
of allowing subordinates in the office to think for
him. He never meddled with the business of

---

[1] At this time the houses which are now No. 10 and No. 12 Downing
Street were the only official residences in that famous purlieu. They
belonged to the Crown, and Bothmar, the Hanoverian Minister, lived
there. When Bothmar died, George II. wished to make Walpole a present
of them. Walpole refused the personal gift, and they agreed that the two
houses should for the future always go with the offices of First Lord of the
Treasury and Chancellor of the Exchequer.

others, and never allowed others to do his own.
Like most, though not quite all great workers, he
was both rapid and methodical. He was con-
trasted by contemporaries with the Duke of Newcastle. The duke was all hurry and confusion,
while Sir Robert, who had ten times the amount
of business, was never in a hurry. " He did
everything with the same ease and tranquillity as
if he was doing nothing."

Walpole was none the less devoted in his application to serious affairs for being a keen sportsman.
George II. expressed his contempt for men of quality
who spent their time in tormenting a poor fox, that
was generally a much better beast than any of
those that pursued him, inasmuch as the fox hurts
no other animal but for his subsistence, while those
brutes who hurt him did it only for the pleasure
of hurting. But he forgave Walpole for this obnoxious relaxation, because all the other eleven
months of the year he gave up to the business of
his prince. Besides his sport in Norfolk, Walpole
hunted with a pack of beagles in Richmond Park;
and it is said of him, as it is of Lord Althorp,
that when the letters arrived he first opened that
from his gamekeeper. It needs not to be added
of such a man, that he was a great sleeper. " I
put off my cares," he said, " when I put off my
clothes."

Walpole's faults of external demeanour were of
a kind of which our own age has become in-
tolerant. His talk at table was such as to-day
would send all the ladies flying from the room.
He had that very sorry vice which Chesterfield
calls his desire to be thought to have a polite and
happy turn for gallantry, and he boasted of his
successes with a coarseness that would now cause
instant expulsion from the mess of any garrison
or any circuit in Great Britain. His extraordinary
laxity in this part of private morality reached to

so incredible a pitch, that he seems to have been
indifferent to the doubtful fidelity of his own
wife, and to the legitimacy of his eldest son's
eldest boy, though the boy was heir to the Walpole
peerage.

Ceremonious people complained of a want of
dignity in Walpole's manners ; it was the natural
consequence of the want of moral dignity in his
character. Policy may have had a share in it.
A hearty kind of frankness, which sometimes
seemed impudence, says Chesterfield, made the
world think that he let them into his secrets, while
the impoliteness of his manners seemed to show
his sincerity. Though he was boisterous in his
ways, and though he appears never to have lost
his Norfolk accent, it is caricature to compare him
with the Westerns and Topehalls of the day. It
is true that Walpole was no scholar and no reader.
" I wish I took as much delight in reading as you
do," he said to a friend after his retirement, " it
would be the means of alleviating many tedious
hours ; but, to my misfortune, I derive no pleasure
from such pursuits." Yet there was nothing
illiterate or uneducated about his speeches. The
standard books contain passages from his great
speech on the Peerage Bill ; they are as far as
possible from the vein of Squire Western. Onslow
says that this performance had as much eloquence
and genius in it as had ever up to that time been
heard in Parliament. The speech on the Triennial
Bill (1734) is a masterpiece of ready invective and
of argument. Chatham declared that the attack
on Wyndham on the occasion of the secession
(1740) was one of the finest speeches he ever heard.
Hervey's report of Walpole's address to his political
friends on the withdrawal of the excise scheme,
shows it to have had not only animation and
energy, but dignity. His political pamphlets are
clear and straightforward statements in sound

English. His reported conversations, and some of his private correspondence, show Walpole to have had both neatness and facility in the trick of Latin quotation. It is true that in one of the best-known parliamentary anecdotes of the time, he once lost a guinea by a blunder in a very familiar verse. He quoted Horace's line as

Nil conscire sibi, nulli pallescere culpae.

Pulteney replied that his Latin was as bad as his logic, and that the right words were *nulla pallescere culpa.* Walpole offered to bet him a guinea. The clerk at the table gave it against the minister, who threw the guinea down. Pulteney, catching it, held it up to the House, calling out, " 'Tis the first money I've had from the Treasury these many years, and it will be the last." The error was no worse than Burke's false quantity when he cried, *magnum vectīgal est parcimonia.* Yet Burke was not illiterate.

Like other charges against Walpole, his offence in shutting the door of patronage in the face of genius has been made far too much of. We have already seen that he procured two hundred pounds a year to the author of the *Night Thoughts.* He offered a pension to Pope, who declined on the ground that he never thought himself so warm in any party's cause as to deserve their money. He subscribed for ten copies of Fielding's works in 1743, though Fielding had abused him. He sent the unfortunate Savage bank-notes. He insisted that Prior, Steele, and Addison had all shown that the most accomplished men of letters make the worst men in affairs ; but to please a friend he made Congreve a Commissioner of Customs, predicting, however, that they would find he had no head for business. It is true that he disappointed the expectations of Swift, and thereby incurred the formidable enmity of that

powerful genius ; but I see no reason why we
should condemn Walpole for leaving the unhappy
man at " wretched Dublin in miserable Ireland." [1]
It is true that he looked upon writing as a mechanical business, and " took up with any pen that he
could find in public offices " ; but Walpole might
well think that when the hack pamphleteer had
pocketed his guineas, all the honour had been paid
that such literature as his deserved.

He cared little more for musicians than he
cared for literature, calling them a pack of fiddlers.
For pictures he had both a genuine enthusiasm
and a good judgment. Many of the noble houses
in Rome, Florence, and Venice were selling their
pictures, and Walpole bought some of the best
of them. Even in the most anxious days of 1742
he took the keenest interest in a Domenichino,
which was too long on its way to England, and
after his fall he alarmed his son by proposing a
jaunt to Bologna, Florence, and Rome to see the
galleries. His collection, or most of it, afterwards
found its way to St. Petersburg, when Walpole's
grandson was driven to raise money on the treasures
of his ancestors, like the Zambccarri and Pallavicini
before him.

Lord Campbell whimsically complains that Walpole is responsible, by his utter neglect of literature and literary men, for giving to official life in
England that " aristocratic feeling and vulgar business-like tone which it has ever since retained." As
if there were any relation between the cause and its
alleged effect. Nobody did less for men of letters
than the younger Pitt, yet no minister ever held,
in transacting public business, a loftier or less
vulgar tone. As for Walpole infecting public life
with aristocratic feeling, it is worth remembering
that he belonged to no great family, and formed
no powerful connections. When men talk of the

[1] Swift, xvii. 17.

Venetian oligarchy of patrician Whigs, they forget
that the patrician oligarchy was controlled in its
palmiest days by a plain country gentleman.
This was one of the taunts most constantly flung
at him by his enemies, as it was a source of just
pride to his own family. Walpole's feeling, in
truth, was much less aristocratic than it was
bourgeois. This was evident long before he reached
the summit of his power. It would have been a
graceful decoration to his solid gifts if Walpole
had played the patron of art and letters ; but
after all the work of government is the despatch of
business, and it is childish to quarrel with a statesman for giving to it a business-like tone. We may
wish that Walpole had lighted up his speeches
and his policy with the language of an elevated
imagination. Still, as his son truly said, his
eloquence was made for use. He had a melodious
voice and little gesture, and is described by contemporaries as an artful rather than an eloquent
speaker, fluent, ready, and vigorous in reply, with
great skill in catching the humour of the House,
and singular clearness in unfolding intricate matters,
making people think that they understood when
they did not. He was right in leaving the declamations of Pitt unanswered, and in thinking
that he had done enough when he had met the
homely contentions of Sir John Barnard. A solid
reply to a solid argument was worth a whole library
of flashy classical references, delusive historical
parallels, and all the rest of the elegant claptrap
which Bolingbroke absurdly called the philosophy
of history. The first qualification in one who
aspires to a ruling place in the counsels of a nation
is, that he should have sound and penetrating
judgment ; the second is ample and accurate
knowledge of the business in hand ; and the third
is tenacity of will and strength of character. All
this is the very root of the matter, and the root of

the matter Walpole had.   The arts of management
were a useful, perhaps an indispensable, adjunct.
Nevertheless, it was not the arts of management
alone or even principally,—it was his practical
grasp of the facts of public business,—that enabled
Walpole to acquire at the same time favour in the
closet of the king, unbounded influence in the
House of Commons, and great, though unhappily
not always unbounded, authority over public opinion
in the country.

Burke rightly contends that Walpole's faults
were superficial.   " A careless, coarse, and over-
familiar style of discourse, without sufficient regard
to persons or occasions, and an almost total want
of political decorum, were the errors by which he
was most hurt in public opinion."   It is certainly
a mistake to dismiss Walpole as a pure cynic.   He
laughed at the patriotic professions of his opponents,
but then they deserved no better.   He refused to
expect too much from men, but this is a virtue,
and not a vice, in one who has to govern men as
they are, and not as the moralist nobly strives to
make them.   Government, like all the practical
arts, means the overcoming of difficulties.   It is
the greatest of the practical arts, because its ends
are the highest, and the difficulties the most subtle,
complex, and incalculable.   The world will never
place Walpole in the highest rank among those
who have governed men, for in the world's final
estimate character goes farther than act, imagination
than utility, and its leaders strike us as much by
what they were as by what they did.   But Walpole
was high enough for his task ; he possessed the
qualities and mastered the maxims that it required.
There are few difficulties, Walpole said in his
letters to Pelham after his own career was closed,
" that cannot be surmounted, if properly and
resolutely engaged in. . . . It is a pity that you
have not time, for time and address have often

carried things that met at the first onset with great reluctance." He was told that somebody had deserted to the Tories after promising that he would always stand by the Whigs. " I advise my young men," Walpole said, " never to use *always*." He had the true political temperament, which makes it possible for a man to be at once intrepid and circumspect. No statesman ever adhered more consistently to all the great articles of his creed ; but, as Hervey says, " he had been too long conversant in business not to know that in the fluctuation of human affairs and variety of accidents to which the best-concerted schemes are liable, they must often be disappointed who build on the certainty of the most probable events ; and therefore seldom turned his thoughts to the provisional warding off future evils which might or might not happen ; or the scheming of remote advantages, subject to so many intervening crosses ; but *always applied himself to the present occurrence*, studying and generally hitting upon the properest method to improve what was favourable, and the best expedient to extricate himself out of what was difficult." Satisfied that he was striving for some broad and honest end, he was not always rigorous as to means. " *He durst do right*," says his son, " *but he durst do wrong too*." Grave and many are the dangers of the courage to do wrong ; yet, on the whole, Walpole must be pronounced to have got discredit for more wrong than he ever did.

The accusation that Walpole was intensely wedded to power, is so little grave as hardly to be an accusation at all. Any man with conscious faculty of strength, and a love of the active business of government, is naturally wedded to power. It may be said that Fox and Burke were strong men, and yet were free from the covetousness of office that consumed men like Walpole and like Pitt. But neither Fox nor Burke ever showed that he possessed remarkable aptitude for carrying on public business ; they were for much too short a time in office to acquire the habit and the passion for it ; and they were never led into temptation by having any real chance of seizing power, after Mr. Pitt once rose above the horizon. A man may be a resplendent rhetorician like Burke, or he may have commanding views on politics like Fox, without being eager for personal power ; but as a rule a practical statesman, conscious of ability for a ruling part in large public transactions, will be as fond of power as Walpole was or as Pitt. Walpole, moreover, like most great ministers, identified his own personality with high objects of national policy ; private triumphs were never separated in his mind from the success of public causes ; and he insisted on having power, because he was convinced that he knew how to use it well. But bad or feeble men, it may be argued, often think the same. The Duke of Newcastle was in his own particular way as fond of power as Walpole. This only shows that the love of power is in itself neither a virtue nor a vice. " My Lord," said Chatham to the Duke of Devonshire, " I am sure that I can save this country, and that nobody else can." There are times when it is a statesman's duty to insist upon power. The only question with which history needs to concern itself is not whether Walpole was intensely wedded to power, but whether his possession and use of it were important for the public good.

Then is it true to say that Walpole was unscrupulous in his means for grasping power and keeping it ? That he gave some advice without a blush which any leading English statesman to-day would readily rather extinguish his public life than give, is unfortunately too certain. Writers on morals tell us that conduct has an aesthetic and an ethical aspect ; it is beautiful or ugly, as well as right or wrong. Walpole's counsels to Queen Caroline, and after her death to the king's own daughters, were indecorous and disgusting, apart from their immorality. It is certain, too, that, as some say, he had not the delicate sense of honour which marks the ideal public man. But it cannot be disguised that many men have shown a want of a fine sense of honour, whom still we should hesitate to brand generally as either unscrupulous or unprincipled. Chatham acted in a way that was not at all to his honour, when he first offered to screen Walpole, and then on his offer being repulsed, redoubled the violence of his attack. George III. did many shabby, cunning, and unscrupulous things, yet tradition is gradually coming to pass him off as a very honest gentleman. Did Mr. Pitt exhibit perfect delicacy of honour when, on coming back to power in 1804, he allowed the stubborn king to ostracise Mr. Fox ? Yet Pitt is usually treated as the pink of moral elevation, and he did undoubtedly take a loftier view of the connection between public authority and private honour than had been the fashion before his time. The equity of history requires that we shall judge men of action by the standards of men of action. Nobody would single out high-mindedness as one of Walpole's conspicuous attributes. It is not a very common attribute among active politicians in any age. On the other hand, Walpole was neither low-minded nor small-minded. His son had a right to boast that he never gave up the interests of his party to serve his own, though he often gave up his own opinions to please friends who were serving themselves. With the firmest confidence in himself, he was neither pragmatical nor arrogant. He was wholly free from spite and from envy ; he bore no malice, though when he had once found a man out in playing tricks, he took care never to forget it ; and he was right, for the issues at stake were too important to allow him to forget.

It is said that he could not brook a colleague of superior ability, and that he took care to surround himself with mediocrities like the Duke of New-castle. We may test the accusation by the conduct of Chatham. Nobody has ever taunted him with this ignoble jealousy, yet he acted precisely as Walpole acted. After fighting against Newcastle as long as he could, he gave way to him just as Walpole had found it expedient to do. " I borrowed the Duke of Newcastle's majority," said Pitt in 1757, " to carry on the public business." It was his majority, not his mediocrity, that Walpole valued. So with the proscriptions. Pitt per-emptorily excluded Henry Fox from his famous administration, though Fox was the ablest debater in Parliament ; and he declined to advance Charles Townshend, who was more near to being his in-tellectual equal than anybody else then in the House of Commons. Neither in Pitt's case nor Walpole's case is it necessary to ascribe their action to anything worse than the highly judicious con-viction that whether in carrying out a great policy of peace like Walpole's, or an arduous policy of war like Pitt's, the very worst impediment that a minister can have is a colleague in his Cabinet who spoils superior ability by perversities of restlessness and egotism. There is not one of the able men ostracised, as it is called, by Walpole, whose political steadiness and personal fidelity he could safely trust; and not one of them, let us not forget to add, who, for fifteen years after his fall, ever showed himself any better able to work with other colleagues and leaders, than he had been to work with Walpole.

Walpole took the pleasures, the honours, the prizes of the world as they came in his way, and he

thoroughly relished and enjoyed them ; but what
his heart was seriously set upon all the time—
seriously, persistently, strenuously, devotedly —
was the promotion of good government and the
frustration and confusion of its enemies. When
men got in his way, he thrust them aside, without
misgiving or remorse, just as a commander in the
field would remove a meddling, wrong-headed, or
incompetent general of division without remorse.
But to be remorseless is a very different thing from
being unscrupulous. I am not aware of a single
proof that Walpole ever began those intrigues
against his enemies, which they were always so
ready to practise against him. It was Stanhope
and Sunderland, not Walpole, who began and
carried out the intrigues that ended in the schism
of 1717. It was Carteret who caballed with the
Tory leaders against his own colleagues after
Sunderland's death. It was Bolingbroke and the
Duchess of Kendal who strove by underhand arts
to procure access for the former to George I., and
when Walpole found out what was going on, he
at once boldly urged the king to grant Bolingbroke
his audience, and to hear all that he had to say. It
was Chesterfield who tried to set up a clique against
Walpole within his own ministry. Much is made
of the case of Townshend. But it is rather a
paradox to prove Walpole's imperious refusal to
share power with able colleagues by referring us to
Townshend, with whom he worked in unbroken
cordiality for the best part of thirty years, and
with whom he did loyally share power, himself in a
relation rather subordinate than otherwise, for
ten of these years. It was Townshend, moreover,
who at the last took advantage of his journey with
the king to Hanover, secretly to ingratiate himself
in the royal favour to the disadvantage of Walpole
at home. Plenty of intriguing was carried on,
but not by Walpole. A candid and particular

examination of the political history of that time, so far as the circumstances are known to us, leads to the conclusion that of all his contemporaries, from men of genius like Bolingbroke and Carteret, from able and brilliant men like Townshend and Chesterfield, Wyndham and Pulteney, down to a mediocre personage like the Duke of Newcastle, Walpole was the least unscrupulous of the men of that time, the most straightforward, bold, and open, and the least addicted to scheming and cabal. He relied more than they did, not less, upon what after all in every age is the only solid foundation of political power, though it may not always lead to the longest terms of office—upon his own superior capacity, more constant principle, firmer will, and clearer vision.

That Walpole practised what would now be regarded as parliamentary corruption is undeniable. But political conduct must be judged in the light of political history. Not very many years before Walpole, a man was expected to pay some thousands of pounds for being made Secretary of State, just as down to a much later date he paid for being made colonel of a regiment. Many years after Walpole, Lord North used to job the loans, and it was not until the younger Pitt set a loftier example that any minister saw the least harm in keeping a portion of a public loan in his own hands for distribution among his private friends. For a minister to buy the vote of a member of Parliament was not then thought much more shameful, than even during the nineteenth century it was thought shameful for a member of Parliament to buy the vote of an elector. Is it a greater sin against political purity to give a member five hundred pounds for his vote, than to advance three thousand for the purchase of his seat? Yet even the austere Pitt laughed, as Walpole might have laughed, at what he called the squeamish and maiden coyness of the House of Commons, in hesitating to admit the right of the owners of rotten boroughs to be compensated for the disfranchisement of their property. It is absurd to suppose that Walpole first tempted mankind into rapacity and selfishness. Even his enemies admitted that corruption had been gaining ground ever since the time of Charles II. Nobody denies that in all its forms, the venality alike of members and of constituencies was vastly worse thirty years after Walpole's disappearance, than anybody ever asserted it to be in his time. To say, with some modern writers, that Walpole organised corruption as a system, that he made corruption the normal process of parliamentary government, that he governed by means of an assembly which was saturated with corruption, is to use language enormously in excess of any producible evidence and of all legitimate inference. It is to attach a weight to the furious and envenomed diatribes of the *Craftsman*, to which the very violence of their language shows them not to be entitled. With unanswerable force it has been asked by Sir Robert Peel and other men of experience in public affairs, how it came about that if Walpole did really corrupt his age, and if the foundation of his strength was the systematic misapplication of the public money to the purposes of bribery, yet a select committee of twenty-one members— nineteen of them his bitter enemies—appointed after his fall to lay a siege to his past life equal in duration to the siege of Troy, produced no specific facts to support the allegations of bribery which had been used every week and every day for so many years to inflame public resentment against him! Two of the great heads of accusation shrank up to miserable dimensions, and the third remained a matter of vague and unsupported inference. Would so lame and impotent a conclusion have been possible if substantial grounds for the accusation had been in existence ?

The charge of undue influence at elections ended in the production of a mere mouse from the labouring mountain. Walpole appears to have promised the mayor a place in the revenue service at Weymouth, in order to secure a returning officer of the right colour ; to have removed some customs officers who declined to vote for the right candidate ; and to have disbursed some petty sums for legal proceedings in boroughs. We find nothing like the lavish purchase of boroughs that was practised wholesale by George III., and which explains the vast debts that loaded the civil list of a king who was personally the most frugal of men. Lord North thought nothing of paying Lord Edgcumbe fifteen thousand pounds for his boroughs, or buying three seats from Lord Falmouth for seven thousand five hundred pounds, though the bargain nearly went off because he would not make the pounds guineas.[1] Walpole never approached such a scale as this.

Nor, again, did the article of conceding fraudulent contracts produce any more appalling disclosure than that in the single case of a not very large contract for payment of troops in Jamaica, the terms had been suspiciously handsome. Finally, the grand accusation of peculation and profusion in the expenditure of the secret service money can be placed no higher than a doubtful inference from a doubtful figure. The committee founded their case on the amount of the secret service money. That amount they pronounced to be so excessive that it could only be explained by a corrupt and improper destination. They took a period for the purposes of comparison, at their own will and pleasure. The secret service money during the ten years from 1707 to 1717 only amounted to three hundred and thirty-eight thousand pounds. The same head under

---

[1] See the *Abergavenny Papers*, printed by the Historical Manuscript Commission. I believe the unprinted portions of the correspondence between George III. and Robinson contain still more astonishing examples of the scale on which the royal boroughmonger went to work.

Walpole's administration from 1731 to 1741 was no less than one million four hundred and forty thousand pounds. Therefore, they argued—and modern writers are content with their argument—a large proportion of the immense expenditure of secret service money in Walpole's government was devoted to the direct purchase of members of Parliament. The premiss, we repeat, can only be accepted with qualifications; next, even if the premiss be taken as offering a precisely just and accurate comparison, the desired conclusion does not necessarily or even reasonably follow from it.[1] The ten years from 1707 to 1717 were arbitrarily chosen; if the first ten years of Anne or of George I. had been taken, the figure would have been much higher, and therefore more favourable to Walpole. The items of the account, moreover, are taken in one way, in order to attenuate the figure of the first period, and in another way, when the object is to expand the figure of the second period; certain payments were charged to the secret service fund in one case, which in the other case had either not been made, or else had gone to another account. The comparative statement is therefore fallacious. Fairly measured, this branch of expenditure, so far as it covered a really secret employment of money which it would be against the interest of the public service to disclose, amounted during ten years of Walpole's administration to less than an annual average of seventy-nine thousand pounds; and that, according to Coxe, is much less than the sum expended for similar purposes during a similar term of years before the Revolution.

Let us, however, suppose that the amount was even higher than this. Why are we to assume as a matter of course that most of it was spent in buying members or boroughs, rather than in the avowed

[1] The reader will find the matter elaborately examined by Coxe in his sixty-first chapter.

objects of buying secret intelligence both at home
and from abroad, and in buying foreign ministers ?
It is certain that Walpole was always singularly
well informed as to the designs of foreign courts.
There were also people at home on whom it was
necessary to keep a still more vigilant eye. The
designs of Jacobite plotters were obscurer and more
intricate than the diplomatic manœuvres of Madrid,
Vienna, or Versailles. Walpole was wisely willing
to pay handsomely for good information about them.
It was said of him that while he was profuse to
his friends, his liberality was literally unbounded to
his tools and spies. Even in our day, no British
minister has ventured to dispense with services of
this odious kind, and every minister still very
properly refuses to account to Parliament or to any
auditor for a shilling of it. That some of this money
went in bribes to members of Parliament, it would
be childish to deny. We shall presently come upon
an instance where nine hundred pounds was paid
to two members of the House of Commons for
their support (below, p. 181). Let us take that as
incontrovertible. But it goes a very little way
towards the broad accusation that we are examining.
The very fact that the king grumbled loudly at a
transaction which cost no more than nine hundred
pounds, shows that such transactions did not usually
mount up to a very large proportion of one hundred
and forty-four thousand pounds a year. The one
detailed case, therefore, that can be adduced to
support the assumption that most of the secret
service money at Walpole's disposal went in parliamentary corruption, itself shows that the assumption is altogether exaggerated and extravagant.
The figures prove too much. We may admit that
the gentlemen who had taken Walpole's money
would be likely to hold their peace about it, and we
know that those who paid the money were authorised
by the king to refuse to give evidence. Yet when

all allowance has been made for these facts, considering how many scores of men must have been concerned, what enormous sums on the hypothesis must have passed, and how passionately ready the great majority of the committee were to procure evidence good or bad at any price, it is surely incredible that, if corruption had been practised on anything approaching to the vast and systematic scale which is so loosely imputed, not one single case should have been forthcoming.

The substance of the charge of corruption is to be sought, not in occasional payment of blackmail to a member or a patron, but in the fact that he reserved the Crown patronage, down to the last morsel, exclusively for members of his own party. He acted on the principle that is accepted in the United States, that is not disavowed in France, and that, although disavowed in Great Britain, has not even yet wholly disappeared there. A member of Parliament who desired anything, from a lucrative office for himself down to a place as tide-waiter for the son of a tenant, knew that his only chance would be to support the administration. The number of offices held by men in Parliament was very great. When Burke introduced his famous scheme of economical reform (1780), he boasted that it would destroy influence equal to the offices of at least fifty members of Parliament. In Walpole's time the number of place-holders at the pleasure of the court must have been considerably in excess of fifty; for the place-bill of 1743 had excluded a certain number of subordinate personages from seats in Parliament. Walpole insisted that all these gentlemen should be sound Whigs. To that extent, acting especially on the owners of boroughs, he systematically affected the disinterestedness and independence of the House of Commons.

Walpole has no doubt suffered much in the opinion of posterity, as the supposed author of

the shallow and cynical apophthegm, that " *every
man has his price.*" People who know nothing else
about Walpole, believe and repeat this about him.
Yet the story is a pure piece of misrepresentation.
He never delivered himself of that famous slander
on mankind. One day, mocking the flowery and
declamatory professions of some of the patriots in
opposition, he insisted on finding self-interest or
family interest at the bottom of their fine things.
" *All these men,*" he said, " *have their price.*" " As
to the revolters," he told the king, " I know the
reasons and I know the price of every one of them."
Nor was he wrong, as time showed. It was not a
general but a particular proposition, and as a particular proposition it was true. When an honest man
came in his way, Walpole knew him well enough.
" I will not say," he observed, " who is corrupt,
but I will say who is not, and that is Shippen."
And yet " honest Shippen " was one of the stoutest
of his opponents.

The absence of any tangible evidence of novel,
extraordinary, lavish, and widespread parliamentary
corruption on Walpole's part, only coincides with
the best positive testimony that we can get. Pitt,
who was one of the most vehement promoters
of the secret committee, five years later publicly
acquitted Walpole of the worst of the charges
brought against him, in terms ample enough to
satisfy the late minister's own sons.[1] Burke, again,
says that it was his fortune to converse with many
of the principal actors against Walpole, and to
examine with care original documents concerning
important transactions of those times (*Regicide
Peace*, i.). His writings, as everybody knows, contain more than one passage showing that he had
informed himself about Walpole's character and
acts ; and in truth much of the great writer's
theoretic wisdom is but the splendid generalisation

[1] Horace Walpole to Mann, 23rd February 1747, ii. 74.

of the great minister's particular policy and practice.
What Burke has to say on the point that we are
now discussing is this:—"Walpole was an honourable man and a sound Whig. He was not, as the
Jacobites and discontented Whigs of his own time
have represented him, and as ill-informed people
still represent him, a prodigal and corrupt minister.
They charged him, in their libels and seditious
conversations, as having first reduced corruption
to a system. Such was their cant. But he was
far from governing by corruption. He governed
by party attachments. The charge of systematic
corruption is less applicable to him, perhaps, than
to any minister who ever served the Crown for so
great a length of time. He gained over very few
from the Opposition."—(*Appeal from New to Old
Whigs*.) Evidence of this kind, coming from a man
of affairs in the generation immediately following,
in contact with some actors in those events and
with many who must have known about them at
first hand, must outweigh any amount of sweeping
presumptions by historians writing a century and a
half after Walpole's fall. The part and proportion
of corruption in Walpole's management of members
is to be gathered from what he did to secure the
rejection of the bill for lowering the interest on the
funds. He got time enough, says Hervey, "to go
about to talk to people, to solicit, to intimidate, to
argue, to persuade, and perhaps to bribe." This
may be taken as a fair example of his usual practice.
Bribery was an expedient in the last resort, and the
appeal to cupidity came after appeals to friendship, to fear, to reason, and to all those mixed
motives, creditable, permissible, and equivocal, which
guide votes in reformed and unreformed parliaments
alike.

The pecuniary affairs of public men are no
concern of the outside world, unless they are
tainted with improbity. So many charges were

made against Walpole under this head, that it is necessary to glance at them. I shall begin with the least serious. Very early in his career of minister Walpole was taunted with abusing his patronage by granting places and reversions of places to his relatives. When his son Horace was little more than a child, he was made Clerk of the Estreats and Controller of the Pipe, with a salary of three hundred pounds a year. At the age of eighteen or nineteen, he became Inspector of Customs; on resigning that post a year later, he was made Usher of the Exchequer, then worth nine hundred pounds a year; and Horace Walpole was able to boast that from the age of twenty he was no charge to his family. The duty of the Usher was to furnish paper, pens, ink, wax, sand, tape, penknives, scissors, and parchment to the Exchequer, and the profits rose from nine hundred pounds a year to an average of double that amount. The post of Collector of the Customs, worth nearly two thousand pounds a year, was granted to Walpole himself, and for the lives of Robert and Edward his sons. The bulk of the proceeds of this patent he devised to his son Horace. In 1721 the minister made his eldest son Clerk of the Pells, with three thousand a year; and in 1739 he gave him the gigantic prize of Auditor of the Exchequer, with a salary of seven thousand pounds. Then when the eldest son resigned the Pells on receiving the Auditorship, the Pells and the three thousand a year went to Edward Walpole, the next brother.[1] All these great patent offices were sinecures; they were always executed by deputy; the principal had not a week's work to do from the first annual quarter-day to the last. We can imagine how these rank abominations would stink in the nostrils of the House of Commons and the

[1] See in Horace Walpole's *Letters*, the *Memorandum respecting his Income*, p. lxxix, and i. 314. Also Coxe, ch. lxi., iv. 320.

Treasury to-day. Yet it is worth remembering that Burke, when he proposed his famous plan of economical reform (1780), though he admitted that the magnitude of the profits in the great patent offices called for reformation, still looked with complacency on an Exchequer list filled with the descendants of the Walpoles, the Pelhams, and the Townshends, and maintained the expediency of these indirect provisions for the families of great public servants. Indirect rewards have long disappeared, and nothing is more certain than that the whole system of political pension, even as a direct and personal reward, is drawing to an end. Whether either the purity or the efficiency of political service will gain by the change, is not so certain. Walpole at least can hardly be censured for doing what, in the very height of his zeal for reform, Burke seriously and deliberately defended.

Abuse of patronage, however, was the least formidable of the charges that descended year after year in a storm on Walpole's head. He was roundly and constantly charged with sustaining a lavish private expenditure by peculation from public funds.[1] The palace which he built for himself in Norfolk was matter for endless scandal. He planted gardens, people said, in places to which the very earth had to be transported in waggons.

---

[1] Thus, in the popular doggerel of the day—

> " But a few years ago,
> As we very well know,
> He scarce had a guinea his fob in ;
> But by bribing of friends,
> To serve his dark ends,
> Now worth a full million is Robin.

> " As oft hath he said
> That our debts should be paid,
> And the nation be eased of her throbbing ;
> Yet on tick we still run,
> For the true sinking fund
> Is the bottomless pocket of Robin."

He set fountains flowing and cascades tumbling, where water was to be conveyed by long aqueducts and costly machines. He was a modern Sardanapalus, imitating the extravagances of oriental monarchs at the expense of a free people whom he was at once impoverishing and betraying. They described him as going down to his country seat loaded with the spoils of an unfortunate nation. He had purchased most of the county of Norfolk, and held at least one-half of the stock of the Bank of England. It was plainly hinted that in view of a possible impeachment at some future day, he had made himself safe by investing one hundred and fifty thousand pounds in jewels and plate as an easily portable form of wealth. He had also secretly despatched four hundred thousand pounds in a single year to bankers at Amsterdam, Vienna, and Genoa, to be ready for him in case of untoward accidents.

These lively fabrications undoubtedly represented the common rumour and opinion of the time, and were excellently fitted to nourish the popular dislike with which Walpole came to be regarded. They had their origin in the same suspicious temper towards an unpopular minister, which two generations before had made the people of London give to Clarendon's new palace in Piccadilly the name of Dunkirk House, and which a generation later prompted the charge that Lord Bute's great house and park at Luton had come out of the bribes of France. They had hardly more solid foundation than the charge of saturating Parliament with corruption. The truth seems to be that Walpole, like both the Pitts, was inexact and careless about money. Profusion was a natural element in a large, loose, jovial character like his, too incessantly preoccupied with business, power, government, and high affairs of state to have much regard for a wise private economy. He was supposed to contribute handsomely towards the expense of fighting elections.[1] He expended in building, adding, and improving at Houghton the sum of two hundred thousand pounds. He built a lodge in Richmond Park at a cost of fourteen thousand pounds. His famous hunting congresses are said to have come to three thousand pounds a year— rather a moderate sum, according to the standard of to-day, for keeping open house for a whole county for several weeks in a vast establishment like Houghton. His collection of pictures was set down by Horace Walpole as having cost him forty thousand pounds more ; but this I suspect to be a very doubtful figure, for, according to a contemporary letter in Nichols's *Literary Anecdotes,* so many of the pictures were presents that the whole cost could hardly have reached thirty thousand pounds ; and it is worth noting that the famous Guido, the gem of the collection, while it cost him some six hundred pounds, was valued in the catalogue when it came to be sold to the Czarina at three thousand five hundred. For all this outlay, his foes contended that the income of his estate and the known salary of his offices were inadequate. They assumed, therefore, that the requisite funds were acquired by the sale of honours, places, and pensions, and by the plunder of the secret service money.

This charitable hypothesis is not really required by the facts, for we have a very tolerable explanation without it. In the first place, rents all over England had gone up by more than one-third, and in some counties they had much more than doubled themselves, since Walpole had come into

---

[1] Coxe (ch. xlv.) quotes from Etough the utterly incredible story that Walpole spent £60,000 out of his private fortune at the general election of 1734. Etough himself, I find, only says that he heard it after Walpole's death from somebody who had good information. The minister may have been profuse, but an expenditure of this magnitude would have been not profusion but insanity ; nor is it at all likely that he was at that time in a position to lay his hands upon so large an amount on his private credit.

his property. As I have stated, when his father
died, in 1700, the rental of the Norfolk estates
was upwards of two thousand pounds. Within
forty years it is computed that it must have risen
to five thousand pounds.[1] Secondly, his wife
brought him a fortune, which cleared the property
of its embarrassments, and presumably left a
margin. Thirdly, his firm and wise conviction of
the folly of the South Sea scheme did not prevent
him from turning his wisdom to account by dealing
in South Sea stock. " I have just sold out," he
said at one moment, " at a thousand per cent,
and I am fully satisfied." [2] Even a moderate
transaction closed at a profit of a thousand per
cent would produce a substantial contribution
towards the building of Houghton or the purchase
of thirty thousand pounds' worth of pictures.
Walpole's success, it should be stated, was not
due to any favour from the South Sea promoters,
such as ruined Aislabie, Craggs, and Sunderland.
They hated him for his unvarying denunciation
of their project, and whatever money he made in
this way was due to his own penetration and the
good information which he got from his own agents.
Fourth, when Walpole died, in 1745, he left a heavy
mortgage on Houghton, and a further debt of fifty
thousand pounds. Fifth, he enjoyed the emoluments of his offices for five - and - twenty years.
This item deserves some examination.

The amount of ministerial salaries in the
eighteenth century is only to be ascertained by
search in the obscure region of the issue books
of the Exchequer, reports of select committees on
finance and committees of inquiry, and various

---

[1] This is Coxe's estimate, but in Mr. Ewald's *Life of Walpole* (published
in 1878) it is stated on the authority of a lately deceased member of the
Walpole family that the rental was understated by Coxe (Ewald, p. 212).
Horace Walpole puts it at a nominal eight thousand pounds a year.
[2] There is a not very intelligible passage in Lady Cowper's *Diary* (p. 144)
about Walpole's speculations.

parliamentary returns of the civil and military establishments.[1] One remark may be made to begin with. During the reign of Queen Anne, and presumably down to a much later date, the modern punctuality of public payments was unknown. A Secretary of State makes light of having to write to a minister abroad apologising for her Majesty's backwardness in paying her servants. A minister at home, he says, can find some resources and make some shift or other to go on, but that those who serve abroad should be in arrears is indeed a great shame.[2] Even the most disinterested of public servants to-day may be startled to find a Secretary of State declaring that he had actually heard nothing of his regular salary for two years.[3] We may safely assume that a Chancellor of the Exchequer at least was able to protect himself against these inconvenient arrears in his own case.

Let us now see how much Walpole drew from the king's purse. From Godolphin's day down to the second administration of the Duke of Portland in 1807 there were invariably five Lords of the Treasury when the Treasury was in commission. The allowance was £8000 a year, which was divided into equal sums of £1600 for each Lord, reduced by various deductions to a net salary of £1220 apiece. But the First Lord, in view of his great responsibilities, received additional pay out of the secret service money, and this addition brought his net emoluments up to £5000 a year. Part payment of the First Lord continued to be made from the secret service money down to 1782, when the king by privy seal made better provision for him by

---

[1] This task has been recently performed by Mr. Edward Hamilton, of the Treasury, a singularly competent hand, and I count myself fortunate in being able to give to my readers the benefit of some of the fruits of his diligent and exact inquiries.

[2] Bolingbroke's *Letters*, March 4, 1712–13.

[3] *Ibid.*, August 7, 1713.

an order that the whole of the salary allowed to the
First Lord should henceforth be received at the
Exchequer. This transfer of salary from secret
service to the civil list in 1782 was followed, as
everybody knows, at the great resettlement of
1831 by its removal to the annual votes submitted
to Parliament. We may take it as reasonably
certain that Walpole received as First Lord the
same sum, including secret service money, as is
to-day voted to the same minister by the House
of Commons. He also received a share of New
Year's gifts, but the amount was trifling. There
is no positive evidence that either the First Lord
or the other Commissioners of the Treasury received
anything out of the fee fund, though it may possibly
have been a practice in those slovenly times for
a First Lord to enrich himself out of perquisites.
This, however, was not all. During the hundred
years preceding Lord Liverpool's administration
in 1812, the First Lord of the Treasury more often
than not was also Chancellor of the Exchequer.
Originally the salary of this office, combined as it
was with that of Under-Treasurer, was no more
than the modest sum of £200. A further addition
of £1600 was made in 1713 " in lieu of perquisites." After being discontinued for three years,
this payment was revived in 1716 in favour of
Sir Robert Walpole, and it afterwards formed a
regular annual charge, bringing the emoluments
of the Chancellor of the Exchequer, as such, up
to £1800 a year. He also received certain fees of
an average value of some £700 a year. The total
annual salary of the Chancellor of the Exchequer
was therefore in Walpole's time about £2400,
and when, as in Walpole's case, this office was held
in conjunction with the post of First Lord, the
total income was about £7400 a year. Walpole,
it may be observed, did not enjoy the salary which
came to Lord North, Mr. Pitt, and Lord Liverpool

as Wardens of the Cinque Ports, and which, having previously to 1778 been from £1100 to £1500 a year, stood between that date and 1827, when it was abolished, at a substantial net figure not much below £3000. While then two of his successors at the head of the Government before the end of the century drew £10,000 a year, Walpole's official income was almost exactly the same as that which was attached to the two offices of First Lord of the Treasury and Chancellor of the Exchequer, when they were held together by the same minister in 1873, and again from 1880 to 1882.[1] To this sum we must add some £2000 a year for the patent place in the Customs, making a gross total of over £9000 a year of public money. Let it be remarked, in conclusion, that the king kept a very tight hand upon the expenditure on secret service, and that the supposition that the minister was free to dip his hand into that fund at his own discretion and pleasure, is a mere misapprehension.

There is nothing unreasonable in supposing that Walpole's official income far exceeded any outlay in which it involved him. For those who exercise themselves in such matters, it is one of the great unsolved mysteries in human annals how it came to pass that Mr. Pitt, who was unmarried, kept no great establishment, gave no sumptuous or costly entertainments, and who drew not much less than two hundred thousand pounds of public money, should yet have died fifty-two thousand pounds in debt. Whatever Pitt's secret may have been, Walpole's circumstances were tolerably clear. His sons were provided for at the public cost; he had a fortune with his wife; he made something of a fortune by speculation; his hospitality was ample, but there

---

[1] The two offices were not combined between 1817 and 1831, except for a few months, when Mr. Canning was both First Lord and Chancellor of the Exchequer. Mr. Perceval is stated not to have drawn the latter salary in 1810–11, when he held both offices.

was no outrageous or unmeasured profusion; he had for twenty years an income from his lands and his offices of thirteen or fourteen thousand a year; and besides debt secured on mortgage, he owed fifty thousand pounds when he died. The account shows that, like so many other great public benefactors, Walpole was no thrifty steward of his private fortunes, but it shows also that his expenditure can be perfectly explained out of known and avowed resources; that the imputation of personal corruption and private plunder —never openly made, be it observed, by any responsible person—is wholly unnecessary, gratuitous, and unsupported; and that the time has come when the reckless calumnies of unscrupulous opponents, striking with masks on, should be at last dropped finally out from the history of a good servant of his country.

CHAPTER VII

THE great constitutional question of the eighteenth century, as every reader knows, was whether the government of the realm should be parliamentary or monarchical. Was it to be an absolute rule of the king; or, as Cromwell sought in the century before, a Parliament making laws and voting money, co-ordinate with the authority of the Chief Person, and not meddling with the executive; or a Parliament containing, nominating, guiding, and controlling its own executive? Walpole found it easiest, safest, and most natural to work steadily towards the last of these three systems. A secondary, but hardly less important question turned on the mechanism by which the system could best be made to work.

Walpole's vehement and effectual resistance to the Peerage Bill proved the strength of his conviction that a close aristocracy was not the system, nor the House of Lords the instrument, for smoothly and successfully conducting the national affairs. The lower House, besides its decisive prerogative of taxation, had the merit, in spite of venal potwallopers and territorial nominees, of containing a considerable representation of the new classes and new interests that were slowly asserting their importance. The large towns, like Bristol and Newcastle, and the freeholders of counties, contributed a strong independent element. Even the immense number of nominees of the great families was probably not out of proportion to their natural weight and influence. In dealing with the House of Commons a minister was dealing with the living and social forces of the country in all their variety. The first question was how to organise them for practical purposes, and Walpole answered it by the principle of Party. He founded his government directly on the support of a Whig majority in the House of Commons, though that majority was in great part due to the assent of powerful members of the House of Lords. The second question was how to keep administration in gear with the party majority, and Walpole's solution was a party Cabinet. The Cabinet system was the key to parliamentary monarchy.

The Act of Settlement did much more than regulate the succession. The Tories consoled themselves by inserting two restrictive constitutional provisions of very remarkable scope. One was an attempt to revive the authority of the Privy Council, by ordaining that all such matters and things pertaining to the government of the realm as are by law and custom properly cognisable in the Privy Council, should be transacted there, and that all resolutions taken there should be signed by such Privy Councillors as should advise and consent to the same. This clause was levelled at the practice which had grown up under Charles II. and his brother, of governing through a select Cabinet of the king's servants, to the detriment, as was supposed, both of the Privy Council as a whole, and of the lawful power and authority of Parliament.

Another provision of the Act of Settlement shows in a still stronger light how little shaped were the constitutional ideas of the day, and has special bearings on Walpole's share in our constitutional development. It enacted that no holder of office under the king should be capable of serving as a member of the House of Commons. A section of only a couple of lines was thus enough, by excluding ministers from the representative House, to divorce the executive from the legislative branch of government. This was by no means in the mind or intention of the framers of the Bill. What they desired was to put a stop to the corruption of members of Parliament by places and pensions from the Crown. The section would have been a remedy for the evil at which it was aimed, but it would have fundamentally transformed the constitution of this country as we understand it, and at the same time all those numerous constitutions which are derived or imitated from our own.

Both clauses were repealed in the early part of the reign of Anne ; they never, therefore, came into operation, but they have an interest of their own in this place. Walpole's work in shaping the constitution may be described as fixing it on the very foundations which the fourth and sixth sections of the Act of Settlement would have made impossible. In other words, the effect of his policy, when it was finally carried through, was to establish the Cabinet on a definite footing as the seat and centre of the executive government, to maintain the executive in the closest relation with the legislature, to govern through the legislature, and to transfer the power and authority of the Crown to the House of Commons. Some writers have held that the first Ministry in the modern sense was that combination of Whigs whom William called to aid him in government in 1695. Others contend that the second administration of Lord Rockingham, which came into power in 1782, after the triumph of the American colonists, the fall of Lord North, and the defeat of George III., was the earliest ministry of the type of to-day.

K

At whatever date we choose first to see all the
decisive marks of that remarkable system which
combines unity, steadfastness, and initiative in
the executive, with the possession of supreme
authority alike over men and measures by the
House of Commons, it is certain that it was under
Walpole that its ruling principles were first fixed
in parliamentary government, and that the Cabinet
system received the impression it bears in our own
time.

This is not the place for any inquiry into the
black-letter learning relating to the various royal
or national councils. The name of Cabinet Council,
according to the books, first occurs casually in
Bacon's *Essays.* Sir Walter Raleigh gave the
name of *Cabinet Council* to his curious collection
of political and polemical aphorisms. As a piece
of mechanism, a Cabinet is first heard of in the
reign of Charles I., and is mentioned by both
Clarendon and Pepys. Charles II. made certain
well-known experiments in the same direction,
but no monarch with Charles's absolutist leanings
could desire to set up any body of private advisers
in an established position, within either the letter
of the law or the spirit of the constitution. The
growth of the Cabinet system has been as gradual,
and as apparently fortuitous, as most other articles
of our constitutional development. Neither the
theory, nor the actual rules and marks of this
peculiar institution, have been put into shape
even by this time ; much less was any theory of
it present to the minds of statesmen in the eighteenth century. The practice was not uniform, and
depended on the cohesion of parties, on the exigencies
of the moment, and on the temper or the position
of the sovereign and of the minister.

It is really in the reign of Queen Anne that the
system comes into pretty clear outline. Godolphin
forced Sunderland upon the queen in 1706, and he

compelled her to remove Harley afterwards. Each of these steps was prompted by the victory of the Whigs in the elections of 1705. So far as it went, this was a recognition of two main principles of the modern system : first, that the chief adviser of the Crown chooses his colleagues ; and next, that a Cabinet depends upon a majority in the House of Commons. But neither principle made very rapid way.

How unsettled were the notions attached to the term of Cabinet, is curiously illustrated in a parliamentary incident of 1711. A motion had been put down, of censure on the Cabinet Council for causing misfortunes in Spain. When the motion came on, the wording was found to have been altered, so as to direct it, not against the Cabinet, but against ministers. The alteration gave rise to a singular discussion. The mover justified it on the ground that the word ministers was better known than the words Cabinet Council. Lord Cowper thought one term just as objectionable as the other : Cabinet was unknown in our law ; both were vague ; the House ought to know what minister was aimed at, and whether more than one was intended. A third speaker held that there was no distinction between Ministry and Cabinet. A fourth replied, truly enough from the modern point of view, that Ministry is more extensive than Cabinet. Peterborough interposed with a witty remark that the Privy Council were such as were thought to know everything and knew nothing, while the Cabinet Council were those who thought that nobody knew anything but themselves.[1]

No fewer than three distinct bodies are to be recognised during the reign of Anne as taking part in the transaction of public business, apart from the deliberations of Parliament on the one hand, and the executive orders of the Secretary of State

[1] *Parl. Hist.* vi. 971.

on the other. First, the treaties of peace and commerce in 1713 are described as having been read in the Great Council, and there ordered to be ratified.[1] This was evidently little more than a merely formal proceeding, without debate, like those of the Privy Council in modern days. It seems that some criticism was offered, but it was resented by Bolingbroke as unusual and meaningless. After the suspicion that had prompted the clause in the Act of Settlement, ministers would hardly have felt themselves safe in ratifying so momentous a set of instruments as the Treaties of Utrecht without this solemnity. A writer of the time, for instance, quoted by Hallam, lays it down that the Chancellor could only make himself safe in setting the great seal to foreign alliances, on condition that a matter of that consequence had been first debated and resolved in council.[2] The whole circumstances of the Peace of Utrecht were so full of peril to the ministers concerned, as later events showed, that the desire to make himself as safe as he could was something very different from the scruple of a constitutional pedant, and simply sprang from natural anxiety to keep his head on his shoulders. There is no reason to suppose that Walpole and the Marlborough Whigs were invited to the Great Council on this occasion, any more than the Opposition is invited on similar occasions now.

Second, mention is frequently made of a body of which all trace has now disappeared. It is called sometimes Committee of Council, and sometimes Lords of the Council, and it met usually at the Cockpit in Whitehall. This body was evidently more restricted than the Privy Council ; it was less restricted than the Cabinet Council, and it was

---

[1] Bolingbroke's *Letters*, 29th September 1713.
[2] See in Lord Campbell's life of Lord King, *Lives of Chancellors*, ch. 125.

different from the Cabinet in composition.[1] It was
perhaps composed with a particular view to collect-
ing the opinion of specialists. Its proceedings were
not purely formal ; it really discussed and transacted business, just as the Cabinet discusses and
transacts it now, and as no other executive body
does now excepting the Cabinet. The preliminary
negotiations of the Treaty of Utrecht were first
disclosed to the Lords at the Cockpit, and repeatedly
debated and authorised by them. Foreign envoys
argued their case before them. They authorised
the instructions to Lord Strafford on his important
mission to the Hague in 1711. They were brought
into action in settling the instructions to Mr. Harley
when he was despatched to Hanover two years later.
We can only conjecture that the Lords of the
Committee of Council were selected by the Secretary of State, with the express approval, possibly
even on the personal initiative, of the queen ; and
were brought together upon occasions of moment,
when it was desired to clothe great executive acts
with peculiar authority and solemnity. The Privy
Council always worked through committees. The
Lords at the Cockpit were probably a committee
especially formed for foreign affairs, just as the
committee where Harley was stabbed by Guiscard
was a judicial committee, taking cognisance of a
charge of high treason. Walpole appointed a committee of the Privy Council to report to Parliament
on the charges of corruption against Lord Maccles-
field. Against this view, however, that the Lords
at Whitehall were a committee on foreign affairs,
analogous to the later committee for trade and
plantations, we have to set the circumstance that

---

[1] In a letter of Bolingbroke's (15th December 1711) he talks of " the
Committee of Council not sitting till to-morrow night, nor the Cabinet
till Monday." They were evidently therefore two distinct bodies. Other
passages in Bolingbroke's letters referring to this Committee of Council
are as follows : 2nd October and 26th October 1711 ; 4th September, 13th
September, 12th November 1713 ; 11th February 1713–14.

it was at a meeting of this Committee of Council, assembled first at the Cockpit, and thence suddenly called to Kensington by the alarming condition of the queen, that the famous scene took place which I have already described (p. 35).[1] So far as I know, there is no later reference to it. Whatever may have been the functions of this committee, it was evidently a ministerial council, and the intrusion of the opposition Lords was an irregularity. The committee may be regarded as a compromise between the old and venerated institution of the Privy Council, and the new, the immature, and the jealously suspected institution of the Cabinet. It is not improbable that Privy Councillors who were not in office sometimes attended this intermediate committee. There are those who believe circumstances to be without difficulty conceivable under which a select body of eminent Privy Councillors might come together to take part in deliberation, and thus might make the chief men of both parties jointly responsible for some great act of state. Speculations of this kind, however, must be viewed with lively suspicion by everybody who believes that party is an essential element in the wholesome working of parliamentary government. Such joint responsibility would destroy party ; and its growth in practice might easily be used both to revive the decaying power of the House of Lords, and even to restore disused authority to any sovereign who might try to press every question in which he happened to feel an interest, towards this method of joint solution.

The third group of advisers was the Cabinet. Down to the end of Walpole's time they are referred to as Lords of the Cabinet or Lords of the Cabinet Council. The Cabinet is now an informal committee

---

[1] The failure to distinguish this body from the Council at large explains the obscurity and confusion of ordinary accounts of what happened on that memorable day.

of the Privy Council, which in time superseded in effect all other deliberative groups formed within that body, and became, as everybody knows, clothed with attributes of its own of the highest novelty and importance. Certain offices, such as that of First Commissioner of the Admiralty,[1] always brought their holder into the Cabinet. So did the Lord-Lieutenancy of Ireland.[2] Some great personages always sat in the Cabinet during the first half of the eighteenth century, who sit there no longer. Lord Chancellor Hardwicke describes a Cabinet Council in 1737, at which the Archbishop of Canterbury was present, as well as the Lord Chamberlain, the Master of the Horse, and the Groom of the Stole. What is still more curious, Bolingbroke, writing to tell the Bishop of Bristol, then Lord Privy Seal and a plenipotentiary at Utrecht, that the queen desires to make him Bishop of London, consoles him for the change by the assurance that as the head of the diocese of London he will keep his seat in the Cabinet.[3] We are no more likely again to see a prelate of the Church in the Cabinet, than we are again to see one made Lord Keeper. When the inclusion of the primate and the great officers of the royal household ceased, it is not easy to tell. In the first Rockingham administration of 1765, the Cabinet contained the Duke of Portland as Lord Chamberlain, and the Duke of Rutland as Master of the Horse. In Pitt's administration which succeeded, the household officers do not appear as of Cabinet rank; and it may be that the great commoner abolished that arrangement. It certainly lasted down to the fall of Walpole.[4]

Some curious expressions linger very late. For

[1] Bolingbroke to Strafford, 12th August 1712.
[2] Stanhope to Walpole, 16th January 1717.
[3] 2nd September 1763.
[4] See Hervey's *Memoirs*, iii. 358 ; Harris's *Life of Hardwicke*, i. 365, 404, etc.

instance, after the Pelhams had routed Granville and Lord Bath in 1746, and when the latter held no office, they made it one of their conditions with the king that Bath "might be out of the Cabinet Council." [1] There could be no question now of the victors in a contest for power bargaining that their defeated rivals should be excluded from attendance at Cabinets as well as from office. Again, it has often been remarked that in the younger Pitt's first Cabinet he was the only commoner; but throughout the eighteenth century Cabinets were mainly composed of peers. It was remarked as an extraordinary proof of Walpole's power that in 1733 he insisted on giving the post of First Lord of the Admiralty to Sir Charles Wager, though no commoner had been thought worthy of that office since the accession of the House of Brunswick. The king made Wager's want of family distinction an express ground of objection, and what is more curious, the veteran himself thought a purely imaginary genealogy a better recommendation than his real services. In Hervey's list of the Cabinet at the close of Walpole's government, Wager and Sir Robert are the only two commoners. In the Pelham government, which after a very short interval succeeded Walpole, Henry Pelham was the only commoner in the Cabinet, and Pelham, like the younger Pitt, was himself the son and the brother of a peer.[2]

A very remarkable incident occurred a few years after Walpole's death. A certain person asserted that he had heard a bishop, the Solicitor-General, and another, drink at table to the health of the Pretender. He was summoned before the Cabinet Council, put on his oath, and interrogated; and after hearing the other side, the Cabinet reported

---

[1] Coxe's *Pelham*, i. 295.

[2] Of this Cabinet we have that rare record, an account of a division, with a list of those who voted aye and no respectively. See the Introduction of Mr. Yorke's *Parliamentary Journal*.

to the king. On this proceeding a debate was raised in the House of Lords, in which strong language was used against what had been done, as a revival of the Star Chamber, the Holy Inquisition, and so forth ; it was no Committee of Council ; it had no more legal authority than any private meeting of lords ; it was an attempt to erect a new jurisdiction. The Lord Chancellor cited an earlier instance of this very extraordinary proceeding, but there seems to be no later.[1]

The same reluctance existed in the first forty years of the century, that has been so constantly felt by wise ministers since, to make precedents for enlarging the Cabinet. The sovereign had much rather confine than extend it, says Bolingbroke. Unfortunately circumstances have set so strongly in the contrary direction during recent years, and the number of ministers almost necessarily included in a Cabinet has grown so large, that it seems as if the result must inevitably be the formation of an interior junto, small enough to allow of deliberation and decision at close quarters. This will be no more than a return to the system of Walpole's time —a large Cabinet, but the effective body composed of himself, the Chancellor, and the two Secretaries of State. Walpole, as we might have expected from his character, called meetings of the Cabinet as seldom as possible. His habit was to invite two or three of his colleagues specially acquainted with the business in hand to dine with him, and then he settled it. The regular Cabinet dinner was an informal device of a later age, marked by the peculiarity and possible convenience that no minute of the topics of discussion was necessarily sent to the sovereign, as in the case of formal meetings of the Cabinet. The Cabinet dinner seems to have been dropped as a practice during the nineteenth century.

---

[1] For a full account see Coxe's *Pelham Administration*, ch. xxx., ii. 254-263.

It was in full vogue during the Aberdeen government, but fell into abeyance under Lord Palmerston, who always cared mainly for national defence and foreign relations, and did not choose to sacrifice a social evening to talk about miscellaneous business.[1]

Perhaps the most important of all the distinctions between the Cabinet in its rudimentary stage at the beginning of the century and its later practice, remains to be noticed. Queen Anne held a Cabinet every Sunday, at which she was herself present, just as we have seen that she was present at debates in the House of Lords. With a doubtful exception in the time of George III., no sovereign has been present at a meeting of the Cabinet since Anne, though George II. presided on one memorable occasion at a meeting of the Privy Council, which is not easily to be distinguished from a Cabinet.[2] This vital change was probably due to the accident that Anne's successor did not understand the language in which its deliberations were carried on. The withdrawal of the sovereign from Cabinet Councils was essential to the momentous change which has transferred the whole substance of authority and power from the Crown to a committee chosen by one member of the two Houses of Parliament, from among other members.

There are other illustrations of the change that has taken place in this direction. For instance Queen Anne herself wrote despatches to her generals and ministers abroad. Again, when Buys, the Dutch Pensionary, came over to argue against the Peace, he had a private audience of the queen, the Secretary of State no doubt being present. The envoy made her a long discourse. She listened to

---

[1] This was Mr. Gladstone's explanation. Mr. Gladstone himself had a Cabinet dinner in Downing Street on the morrow of the defeat at the election of 1886, and business was discussed in the regular way.

[2] Lord Waldegrave in his *Memoirs* mentions a meeting of "the king's principal servants," to consider the Prince of Wales's establishment in 1756. Some of the books take his language to mean that the king was present, but the implication is clearly the other way.

him with great patience, told him that the burdens of the war were too heavy to be longer borne, and desired him to confer with her ministers, meaning, however, the Committee of Council, and not ministers in Cabinet.[1] Maffei had a similar interview on the part of Savoy. No foreign envoy would now attempt to address the sovereign personally upon national business, though the distinctive mark of an ambassador is that he is, and a minister is not, entitled to personal access to the sovereign. In modern practice, when the Secretary of State introduces an ambassador, it is the Secretary who breaks the seal of the letter of credit before the ambassador presents it to the sovereign.[2]

Passing from the sovereign to her ministers, we find the relations of the Secretary of State to the Cabinet, at least during the negotiations of the Peace of Utrecht, such as would now be held distinctly unconstitutional. St. John, when Secretary of State, invites the British representatives abroad to keep up a double correspondence with him, and to write not merely " letters containing the general thread of business which are read in Cabinet," but also private letters with such secret particulars as may not be properly communicated even to the Cabinet till the queen should think fit. He explains as one of the advantages of these personal letters that the minister is under no obligation to leave

[1] Bolingbroke's Correspondence, 23rd October 1711.
[2] In the Harcourt Papers there is a letter from Prior to Lord Harcourt (March 21, 1715):

MY LORD—As I have been particularly concerned in a negotiation at present so much questioned, and done my best in the execution of the commands of my superior ; and as I have received advices alarming enough, I desire your advice particularly as to the point of my first coming into France with no other power than that of the Queen, with her own private *cachette*, if this were not in law a sufficient warrant for my acting. Pray give credit to what these gentlemen will say to you on my part.
And believe me ever with great respect yours   M. PRIOR.

Here is the queen's private *cachette* :—"Commission donnée au Sieur Prior. Anne R. Le Sieur Prior est pleinement instruit et autorisé de communiquer à la France nos demandes préliminaires et de nous en rapporter la réponse.—Signé, A. R." (Harcourt Papers, ii. 09.)

them behind him in his office.[1] No doubt, private and unofficial correspondence of that kind is still a common channel of important information, but no minister would deliberately hide it from his colleagues for purposes of his own, as Louis XV. worked his sinister system of double correspondence against his own servants. Bolingbroke goes much further. He even sends to the ambassador the project of the Peace, without having communicated it to the Cabinet.[2] The memorable decision to create twelve peers in a day was taken without reference to the body, whose collective assent to so momentous a step would to-day be regarded as not any less indispensable a preliminary than the assent of the sovereign herself.[3]

It is easy to see to what point the evolution of Cabinet government was brought in Walpole's time and by his influence. Two circumstances were essential to the growth of this form of government in the British type. One was the absence of the sovereign, of which I have already spoken. How great a difference that makes, was shown by the effect of Louis XVIII. and Louis Philippe sitting at the head of the table, as the President of the French Republic now does, while their ministers discussed business. The second essential is the presence of ministers in the legislature. The founders of the American constitution, as all know, followed Montesquieu's phrases, if not his design, about separating legislature from executive, by excluding ministers from both Houses of Congress. This is fatal to any reproduction of the English system. The American Cabinet is vitally unlike our own on this account. If Walpole had taken the line afterwards adopted at Philadelphia, ministerial responsibility would have borne a very different sense from that with

[1] To Lord Bath, 8th May 1711.
[2] 6th April and 6th May 1711.
[3] To Strafford, 1st January 1711.

which we are now so familiar, as almost to regard
it as of divine ordinance. In no direction did
Walpole give a more important turn to our affairs.
He imparted a decisive bias at a highly critical
moment; though the struggle was a long one, it
is to Walpole more especially that we owe it that
government in England is carried on, not by royal
or imperial ministers, as in Prussia, nor by ministers
not sitting in the legislature, as in the United States,
but by parliamentary ministers. In this view the
reader will perhaps not regard it as an irrelevant
digression, if we devote a page or two to recalling
what government by parliamentary ministers is, and
how it is worked.

The principal features of our system of Cabinet
government to-day are four. The first is the
doctrine of collective responsibility. Each Cabinet
minister carries on the work of a particular department,[1] and for that department he is individually
answerable. When Pitt's administration came to
an end in 1801, and Lord Loughborough was
displaced from the woolsack, the ex-Chancellor, to
the amazement of the new Prime Minister, kept
the key of the Cabinet boxes, and actually, without
being summoned, attended meetings of the Cabinet.
At last Addington wrote to beg him to discontinue
his attendance, on the principle that " the number
of the Cabinet should not exceed that of the persons
whose responsible situations in office require their
being members of it." In addition to this individual
responsibility, each minister largely shares a collective responsibility with all other members of the
government, for anything of high importance that
is done in every other branch of the public business

---

[1] There are cases of a minister without a portfolio, e.g. Lord Lansdowne
sat in the Coalition Cabinet of Aberdeen without a department, and Lord
John Russell led the House of Commons through the session of 1853
without holding any office ; but they are too rare to affect the general
description, and parliamentary sentiment is likely to prevent them from
ever becoming normal.

besides his own. The question whether the mistakes or misdeeds of one minister involve all the rest, is of course not quite independent of the position of the minister, or of the particular action. The censure and impeachment of Lord Melville, for example, was so purely personal in its bearings that it did not break up the government of Mr. Pitt. Lord Ellenborough again, resigned in 1858, in order to save his colleagues from a vote of censure for publishing his despatch to the Governor-General of India. But as a general rule every important piece of departmental policy is taken to commit the entire Cabinet, and its members stand or fall together. The Chancellor of the Exchequer may be driven from office by a bad despatch from the Foreign Office, and an excellent Home Secretary may suffer for the blunders of a stupid Minister of War. The Cabinet is a unit—a unit as regards the sovereign, and a unit as regards the legislature. Its views are laid before the sovereign and before Parliament, as if they were the views of one man. It gives its advice as a single whole, both in the royal closet and in the hereditary or the representative House. If that advice be not taken by the elective House, provided the matter of it appear to be of proper importance, then the Cabinet, before or after an appeal to the electors, dissolves itself and disappears. The first mark of the Cabinet, as that institution is now understood, is united and indivisible responsibility.

The second mark is that the Cabinet is answerable immediately to the majority of the House of Commons, and ultimately to the electors whose will creates that majority. Responsibility to the Crown is slowly ceasing to be more than a constitutional fiction, though even as a fiction it possesses many practical conveniences. William IV., it is true, dismissed the Melbourne government in 1834 of his own motion, and Sir Robert Peel stuck to the helm for his hundred days in spite of a hostile majority. But though such experiments may by bare possibility recur, they will hardly recur often, and they will never last long.[1] The only real responsibility is to the House of Commons. Responsibility to the House of Lords means no more than that that House may temporarily resist bills of which it disapproves, until the sense of the electors of the House of Commons has been taken upon them. Even in Walpole's time, when the House of Lords passed a motion of censure upon the Spanish Convention in 1739, the minister paid no attention to it.[2]

Third, the Cabinet is, except under uncommon, peculiar, and transitory circumstances, selected exclusively from one party. There have been coalitions of men of opposite parties, but in most cases, down to the present time, coalition has been only

[1] The *Melbourne Papers* show clearly enough that the proceeding of 1834 was not without something very like instigation from Lord Melbourne himself; but it was accepted as an act originating with the king, and must be regarded as something the Crown could do in 1834. On the general view in this paragraph, an important criticism has been made by a high authority. It is contended that if we observe the experiences of parliamentary government in the Colonies, we shall find that the Crown (through the Governor) exercises powers which may not be so often exercised at home, but which are no less possessed here, and should not be lightly regarded as obsolete. The Crown (Governor) has under his view a Cabinet, an elected assembly, and an electorate ; and it may be the duty of the Governor (Crown) to refuse a dissolution or to insist upon a dissolution :— to refuse a dissolution when the election of the assembly has been recent and there is no sign of any variation between the dominant mind of the new assembly and the mind of the electorate, and the claim for a new dissolution seems only the desperate throw of beaten ministers ; on the other hand to insist upon a dissolution when there is firm, assured, and accumulated evidence of a divergence amounting to direct contradiction between the assembly and the electorate. Of course, there must be ministers ready to adopt the will of the Crown, and to become responsible for it as their own. But is it not most desirable that, while exercised with extreme care and delicacy, this power of securing that Cabinet, assembly, and electorate are in genuine accord, should not be lost ? Might not such a power serve as the equating force of parliamentary government, far better than incessant elections to which we might otherwise drift ? To the present writer it seems that no friend of monarchy, at any rate, will be in a hurry to give to these questions an affirmative answer. The whole case assumes the existence of passion and collision, the action of the king or queen would inevitably please one side and displease the other ; and the hereditary foundation of the royal power (in this respect unlike the power of a colonial Governor) would be a weakness and a danger.

[2] Coxe, iv. 58.

the preliminary of fusion. There have been conjunctions, again, of men openly holding directly opposite opinions on subjects going to the very foundations of government, and turning on the very principles that mark party difference. Lord Liverpool's ministry, for instance, lasted for fourteen years, with so important an issue as Catholic emancipation left an open question. But notwithstanding both coalitions and open questions, it remains generally true that Cabinets are made from one party.[1]

Fourth, the Prime Minister is the keystone of the Cabinet arch. Although in Cabinet all its members stand on an equal footing, speak with equal voice, and, on the rare occasions when a division is taken, are counted on the fraternal principle of one man, one vote, yet the head of the Cabinet is *primus inter pares*, and occupies a position which, so long as it lasts, is one of exceptional and peculiar authority. It is true that he is in form chosen by the Crown, but in practice the choice of the Crown is pretty strictly confined to the man who is designated by the acclamation of a party majority. If a party should chance to be divided or uncertain as to its leader, then undoubtedly the favour of the Crown might suffice to turn the balance. There might be some exaggeration in saying that the veto of the Crown on a First Minister is virtually as dead as its veto on a bill; still the Crown could hardly exercise any real power either of selection or of exclusion against the marked wishes of the constituencies.

The Prime Minister, once appointed, chooses his own colleagues, and assigns to them their respective offices. It sometimes happens that, in the case of very important colleagues, they are almost as effectually designated to him by public opinion and

[1] No serious qualification is made in this statement by the fact that when George III. was suffering from his first dangerous attack of illness, Pitt summoned the whole Privy Council to receive a report as to the king's situation, without distinction of party, and of the 54 members who attended (Dec. 3, 1788), 24 belonged to the Opposition (see Stanhope's *Pitt*, i. 403).

parliamentary position, as he is himself designated to the sovereign for his own high office. Still, there is more than a margin for his free exercise of choice in the persons admitted to his Cabinet, and in all cases it is for him alone to settle the distribution of posts. Constitutional respect for the Crown would inspire a natural regard for the personal wishes of the sovereign in recommendations to office, but royal predilections or prejudices will undoubtedly be less and less able to stand against the Prime Minister's strong view of the requirements of the public service.[1]

The flexibility of the Cabinet system allows the Prime Minister in an emergency to take upon himself a power not inferior to that of a dictator, provided always that the House of Commons will stand by him. In ordinary circumstances he leaves the heads of departments to do their work in their own way. It is their duty freely and voluntarily to call him into council, on business of a certain order of importance. With the Foreign Secretary he is in close and continuous communication as to the business of his office. Foreign affairs must always be the matter of continuous thought in the mind of the Prime Minister. They are not continuously before the Cabinet; it has not therefore the same fulness of information as the Prime Minister; and consequently in this important department of public action, the Cabinet must for the most part, unless there be some special cause of excitement, depend upon the prudence and watchfulness of its head.[2]

---

[1] "Viscount Melbourne must distinctly declare that, whilst he trusts he is incapable of recommending to your Majesty any individuals whose character and conduct appear to him to disqualify them from holding any situation of trust and responsibility, he can neither admit nor acquiesce in any general or particular exclusion, and that he must reserve to himself the power of recommending for employment any one of your Majesty's subjects who is qualified by law to serve your Majesty" (Lord Melbourne to William IV. (1835), *Melbourne Papers*, 274). The desired exclusions were O'Connell, Sheil, and Joseph Hume.

[2] Perhaps I have been led to make rather too much of the relations between Prime Minister and Foreign Secretary, from the views and

In case of differences arising between departments, it is to the Prime Minister that the appeal lies, and the regular course for a minister who is dissatisfied with his chief's decision is to retire. Where the Prime Minister is displeased with the language or the action of a colleague, he possesses, indeed, no direct prerogative to call for his resignation, without going first to the sovereign and procuring the royal assent. But that assent could practically never be refused to a Prime Minister with a parliamentary majority, unless the sovereign were prepared to take new advisers and face a dissolution. Though it is just conceivable that the sovereign might remonstrate successfully against the minister's request for a colleague's dismissal, yet it is not likely that a minister would make a request of such moment without intending to abide by it and to press it to the end.

An important qualification of the Prime Minister's power exists in the case of the Crown. Here it is well understood that the sovereign has a right to demand the opinion of the Cabinet as a court of appeal against the Prime Minister or any other minister. It is now publicly known, for instance, that in the difficult foreign crisis of 1859–61 despatches were frequently referred back by the sovereign from the Foreign Secretary and the Prime Minister to the Cabinet as a whole, and were there constantly modified in the sense desired. This is clearly a practical power left to the Crown, and if there chanced to be a strong Cabinet, the use of such a power might result in a considerable reduction of the Prime Minister's normal authority, and its transfer to the general body of his colleagues.[1]

practice of Mr. Gladstone. Those relations are likely to be close, but the degree of closeness will depend upon the gravity of foreign affairs at a given time, and on the interests and disposition of the two men.

[1] This was Mr. Gladstone's view. On the other hand Lord Broughton's diaries report on this occasion a rather heated discussion in the Cabinet

In filling up the highest posts within a department, such as the headship of the permanent staff, the nomination of an ambassador, or the appointment to the governorship of an important colony or the great dependency of India, the Prime Minister, though not taking the initiative, would still usually expect to be consulted by the minister more directly concerned. Even the Lord Chancellor is believed sometimes to go through the form of consulting him in filling vacancies on the judicial bench. Finally, just as the Cabinet has been described as being the regulator of relations between Sovereign, Lords, and Commons, so is the Prime Minister the regulator of relations between the sovereign and his servants. " As the Cabinet stands between the sovereign and Parliament, so the Prime Minister stands between the sovereign and the Cabinet." [1] This does not mean that any minister is out of immediate communication with the Crown, in matters strictly affecting his own department as to which the Crown may desire to be informed ; but only that outside of these matters it is the Prime Minister only who conveys to the sovereign the views of his colleagues. Such attempts to intrigue with the sovereign against a colleague as were common with Sunderland, Stanhope, Townshend, and Carteret, and as were long afterwards repeated with particular baseness by Lord Loughborough, when he secretly warned George III. of Pitt's Catholic policy and advised him against it, are, we may be very confident, never likely to recur.

Here this too long digression may end. Hardly one of these four principles was accepted by Walpole, or by anybody else in his time, with the

---

as to the queen's complaints of Palmerston. They all rejected the idea that the queen could constitute the Cabinet a court of appeal against the Prime Minister or the Foreign Secretary. George III. in January 1784 expressly desired Mr. Pitt to arm himself with the opinion of the Cabinet, or as he called them, " the confidential Ministers " (see Stanhope's *Pitt*, i. Appendix, pp. iv-vi).

[1] Mr. Gladstone's *Gleanings*, i. 236, etc.

accuracy or the fulness with which they are all
acted upon at present. They all coloured and shaped
the new form that popular government was putting
on, but neither the joint solidarity of the Cabinet,
nor its direct responsibility as the servant of Parliament, had yet approached maturity. Walpole
undoubtedly made a long stride towards establishing the doctrine of Cabinet solidarity. When he
pressed for the dismissal of the Duke of Roxburghe
in 1725, he did so on the ground that " the present
administration is the first that was ever yet known
to be responsible for the whole government, with
a Secretary of State for one part of the kingdom who, they are assured, acts counter to all
their measures." Yet when Carteret made his
famous motion for Walpole's removal in 1741, Lord
Wilmington, though he held the office of Privy
Seal, did not vote in Walpole's defence against
the motion. The cardinal question of the position
of the Prime Minister was in a most singular
stage, for Walpole was in practice able to invest
himself with more of the functions and powers
of a Prime Minister than any of his successors,
and yet was compelled by the feeling of the time
earnestly and profusely to repudiate both the name
and title, and every one of the pretensions that it
involves.

The earliest instance in which I have found the
head of the government designated as the Premier
is in a letter to the Duke of Newcastle from the
Duke of Cumberland in 1746, though in Johnson's
Dictionary, published nine years later, *premier* still
only figures as an adjective. The king wished
Pitt, then just made Paymaster, to move the
parliamentary grant to the victor of Culloden.
" I should be much better pleased," writes the
Duke of Cumberland, " if the Premier moved it,
both as a friend and on account of his weight.
I am fully convinced of the Premier's goodwill to

me." [1]   On the other hand, in a debate so late as
1761, George Grenville declared that Prime Minister
is an odious title, and he was sorry that it was
now deemed an essential part of the constitution.
Lord North is said never to have allowed himself
in his own family to be called Prime Minister.

A flood of light is shed upon the advance that
was made in the conception of this organ in government, by comparing Walpole's professions before
the middle of the century, with those of Mr. Pitt
at the end of it. Pitt's view of the position of the
Prime Minister was stated in the well-known letter
of Lord Melville to Addington in 1803. Addington
had absurdly suggested that Mr. Pitt should return
to the government either as Secretary of State or as
Chancellor of the Exchequer. Lord Chatham was
to be the head of the administration. As might
have been expected, the man who had for nearly
twenty years been at the head of affairs in times
of unexampled emergency, laughed at the proposal.
He said satirically that he really had not the curi-
osity to ask what office he was to fill. He desired
Lord Melville, however, to explain his views to
Addington. Mr. Pitt, wrote Lord Melville, " stated
not less pointedly and decidedly his sentiments
with regard to the absolute necessity there is in
the conduct of the affairs of this country, that
there should be an avowed and real minister,
possessing the chief weight in the council, and
the principal place in the confidence of the king.
In that respect there can be no rivalry or division
of power. That power must rest in the person
generally called the First Minister, and that minister
ought, he thinks, to be the person at the head of
the finances. He knows, to his own comfortable
experience, that notwithstanding the abstract truth

[1] Coxe's *Pelham Administration*, i. 486. The Duchess of Marlborough
in her Correspondence frequently speaks of " the Premier Minister," but
never of "the Premier" (vol. ii. 152, 181, etc.). First use of "Prime
Minister," see Anson, ii. 118.

of that general proposition, it is noways incompatible with the most cordial concert and mutual exchange of advice and intercourse amongst the different branches of executive departments; but still, if it should come unfortunately to such a radical difference of opinion that no spirit of conciliation or concession can reconcile, the sentiments of the minister must be allowed and understood to prevail, leaving the other members of administration to act as they may conceive themselves conscientiously called upon to act under the circumstances." [1]

What Pitt here arrogates to the minister as his just claim and demand, Walpole was obliged to thrust away from himself as a reproach and an offence against the constitution of the realm. When the great attack was opened upon him in 1741, Carteret expressly described as one of his worst misdemeanours, that he had usurped the sole power of directing all public affairs, and recommending to all public posts, honours, and employments. It was repeated as an article of charge against him in every speech, that he solely enjoyed and engrossed the ear of his sovereign. They called him a second Strafford, who excluded every man that disdained to be his slave from the pay and even from the smiles of the court. Mr. Sandys, who led the attack in the Commons, declared that: "According to our constitution we can have no sole and prime minister; we ought always to have several prime ministers or officers of state; every such officer has his own proper department; and no officer ought to meddle in the affairs belonging to the department of another." In arrogantly despising this fundamental principle, Walpole had been guilty of a most heinous crime against the constitution. The attack was repulsed in both Houses, but the minority in the Lords

[1] Stanhope's *Life of Pitt*, iv. 24.

drew up a protest, and the opening clause in it
runs thus : " We are persuaded that a sole, or
even a First Minister, is an officer unknown to the
law of Britain, inconsistent with the constitution
of this country, and destructive of liberty in any
government whatsoever."

In Walpole's defence, neither he, nor any of
those who spoke for him, contradicted this principle ; they only denied the allegations of fact. The
Bishop of Salisbury could find no proof that Walpole
had usurped the authority of First Minister. The
Lord Chancellor put his apology for Walpole's
interference in patronage no higher than that, as
there happened to be a very good correspondence
among his Majesty's ministers, applicants for places
came to Walpole, not because he had the ear of the
king, but as the shortest way to the ear of the
minister who had the place to give away. Walpole
himself paid little attention to this particular
charge in his reply, but in deprecating it he took
up a remarkable position, to which neither Mr.
Pitt nor any of his successors would have assented.
" I do not pretend," he said, " to be a great master
of foreign affairs ; in that post it is not my business
to meddle ; and as one of his Majesty's council,
I have only one voice." Notwithstanding this
disclaimer, Walpole was undoubtedly an example
of the important political truth, of which Mr. Pitt
and Sir Robert Peel are equally conspicuous illustrations, that no administrations have been more
successful than those where the distance in parliamentary authority, party influence, and popular
position, between the Prime Minister and his colleagues in the Cabinet, has been wide, recognised,
and decisive.

In concluding this portion of my subject, it is
proper to remark that it would be very misleading
to take the arrangements of any one period, whether
1889 or 1740 or any other date, as being definitely

fixed parts of the constitution. To-day it is correct to say that the Cabinet has drawn to itself all, and more than all, of the royal power over legislation, as well as many of the most important legislative powers of Parliament. It is possible that within the next hundred years government by Cabinet may undergo changes of substance as important as the changes since the time of Sir Robert Walpole ; but it is worthy of remark that the statesman of widest experience and highest authority in the working of our constitutional system during the greater part of the reign of Queen Victoria, declared that in his judgment the Cabinet as a great organ of government has now found its final shape, attributes, functions, and permanent ordering.

EXTRACT FROM *NOTES AND QUERIES* (9th S. iii. Feb. 11, 1899)

" PRIME MINISTER

" Every additional investigation confirms the opinion that, while both ' Prime Minister ' and ' Premier Minister' were earliest applied to Harley, and were expressly drawn from French usage, ' Prime Minister' was first generally given as an official title to Walpole and ' Premier ' to the younger Pitt. It is of special interest in this connexion to note that Sir John Vanbrugh, architect and dramatist, whose use of ' First Minister ' in comedies of 1697 and 1705 I have mentioned (*ante*, p. 15), wrote on 26 Nov., 1723, to Lord Carlisle, upon the death of the French Regent :—

" ' The Duke of Bourbon was designed by the late Duke of Orleans to be prime minister in his room very soon, the fatigue being too much for him ; so he was immediately declared upon this account.'—' Historical MSS. Commission Fifteenth Report,' Appendix, pt. vi. p. 46.

" But on 30 Dec., 1727, Lady E. Lechmere wrote to the same peer from ' Twitneham ' that

" ' our Premier, who is now hunting a hind in the neighbourhood, is in as great favour with the King as with the Queen, and in all appearance will continue so.'—*Ibid.*, p. 53.

" While almost exactly two years later Lady Mary Howard told her father of the quarrel between Lord Townshend and Sir Robert Walpole, with the comment :—

" ' John Malcoat's place in my opinion is a much happier situation in life than a first Minister's.'—*Ibid.*, v. 62.

" We thus have it established that, although the usage of any such special term was tentative and varying, ' Premier ' was applied to Walpole, and as early as 1727 ; but it took far longer than ' Prime Minister ' to come into common use. Before, however, Burns had spoken of Pitt as ' yon Premier Youth,' George Selwyn had written, on 25 November, 1775, to another Lord Carlisle than the one previously mentioned, a note saying :—

" ' There is certainly no immediate prospect of a change at home. . . . I think that there is more reason to apprehend a disunion at home from the Premier and the new Secretary [Lord North and Viscount Weymouth] than from any other circumstances whatsoever.'—*Ibid.*, p. 749.

"And on 13 March, 1782, Selwyn further wrote to the peer during the keen political crisis which ended in the fall of Lord North :—

" ' Young Pitt will not be subordinate ; he is not so in his own society. He is at the head of a dozen young people, and it is a corps separate from that of Charles's [Fox] ; so there is another premier at the starting-post, who, as yet, has never been shaved.'—*Ibid.*, p. 593.

" This forecast was remarkably fulfilled ; but what is even more interesting is that its fulfilment ultimately secured a definition of the position of Prime Minister, assented to by two of the leading statesmen of the day, and worthy of being placed upon special record. After the bitter dispute between Pitt as Premier and Lord Fitzwilliam as Lord Lieutenant of Ireland, there was drawn up in March, 1795, an ' explanation settled between Mr. Grattan and Mr. Burke, coming from Lord F[itzwilliam] and the Chancellor ' (Lord Loughborough) ; and this document thus commenced :—

" ' They stated that Lord F.'s view was : " To support in Ireland the English Government, considering Mr. Pitt as *the Prime Minister,* without whom no material measure as to *things* or *persons* is to be concerted or done—not setting up a Government of Departments, but that each department acting *under* him should meet with its due and honourable support *from* him." '—*Ibid.*, p. 722.

" This definition of the supreme position of what Lord Carlisle, with the memorandum then in his possession, described as ' the King's Prime Minister ' (*ibid.*, p. 725), is of constitutional value ; and its spirit has certainly been accepted by most Premiers since Pitt.

" Alfred F. Robbins."

CHAPTER VIII

FISCAL POLICY

WHEN historians blame Walpole for not attempting
reforms, they lose sight of a leading chapter in his
policy : they omit his vigorous and fruitful efforts
in the field of trade and commerce, which was then
of far greater national importance than any merely
political or parliamentary changes. His biographer
is in the right when he complains that men have
thought too exclusively of the minister's triple
alliances, quadruple alliances, and foreign treaties ;
have made too much of the charges of ambition
and corruption brought against him by unbridled
faction ; and have left those salutary regulations
which ought to render the name of Walpole dear
to every Englishman, to be principally confined to
books of rates and taxes.[1] Walpole opened this
chapter in what was, for the time, a remarkable
proposition. In 1721 the king's speech contained
a paragraph foreshadowing reforms, compared with
which bills for abolishing places or shortening
parliaments were but as flies on the legislative
wheel. " We should be extremely wanting to
ourselves," the king was made to say, " if we
neglected to improve the favourable opportunity
given us of extending our commerce, upon which
the riches and grandeur of this nation chiefly
depend. It is very obvious that nothing would
more conduce to the obtaining so public a good,

---

[1] Coxe, ch. xxii.

than *to make the exportation of our own manufactures, and the importation of the commodities used in the manufacturing of them, as practicable and as easy as may be.*" Harley and Bolingbroke had made an ineffectual opening in the direction of free trade, in the abortive treaty of commerce with France at the time of Utrecht;[1] and to that extent Lord Beaconsfield was justified in a favourite contention of his responsible days, that peace and free trade were the original property of Tory statesmen. But the royal speech of 1721 is the first full, general, and distinct approach, so far as I know, made by an English statesman towards those enlightened views of trade which were fifty-five years later given in systematic shape to the world by the genius of Adam Smith. Walpole was as good as his word ; he persuaded Parliament in the session of 1721 to remove duties on export from one hundred and six articles of British manufacture, and duties on import from thirty-eight articles of raw material.

Nine years later (1730) he conferred a more indisputable boon on the trade with Georgia and Carolina. The narrow policy of those times restricted the colonies to an exclusive intercourse with the mother country. Walpole passed an Act allowing the Carolina and Georgian planters to export their rice direct to any port in Europe south of Finisterre, provided they sent it in British ships, manned by British sailors. The result was that the rice of the American plantations beat the rice of Egypt and northern Italy out of the markets of Europe. Shortly before his fall, he carried a measure for allowing the West Indian traders to export sugar direct to foreign countries, provided it were in British bottoms, without first landing it

---

[1] It has been pointed out that Arthur Moore, a commissioner of plantations, who was the real author of Bolingbroke's commercial treaty with France, had become, on Bolingbroke's return in 1725, a close ally of Walpole (R. Harrop's *Bolingbroke*, pp. 149 and 245).

in British ports. The growth of colonial trade was
one of the most striking facts of Walpole's time.
A dozen years before he went to the Treasury
the whole trade with the plantations — about
£1,300,000, both export and import—was only a
few thousand pounds more under the head of
export, and it was a third less in import, than that
which was carried on with Jamaica alone, five-
and-twenty years after Walpole left the Treasury.
In the same interval, the total export trade from
England with all the world had risen from six
million pounds a year to more than twelve millions.[1]

These were not mere hand-to-mouth expedients,
but the outcome of enlightened and comprehensive
views. Shortly after the failure of the excise
scheme, which I shall have next to describe, a
retired deputy-governor of Virginia came over to
Walpole with a plan for an American tax. " No,"
said the minister, " I have old England set against
me, and do you think I will have the new England
likewise ? " A few years later (1739) the temptation was renewed. Walpole again repelled it. His
object had always been, he said, to encourage
colonial commerce, because the greater the pros-
perity of the colonies, the greater would be their
demand for English goods ; and that was the true
way in which to turn colonies into a source of wealth
to a mother country. Walpole was content with
seeing that no trouble came from America. He
left it to the Duke of Newcastle, and the duke left
it so much to itself, that he had a closet full of
despatches from American governors which had
lain unopened for years. This was what Burke
described as treating the colonies with salutary
neglect, and what caused it to be said that George
Grenville lost America because he was foolish
enough to read the American despatches.

The most famous of all Walpole's projects in

[1] Burke's *Observations on the Present State of the Nation.*

taxation, in the sense of being that which made most noise, was the scheme for extending the excise. This gave his enemies their first serious advantage over him, and inflicted on his power the first important check. In itself the new policy of excise offered no striking or imposing features. The most important element of it, the facility for warehousing imported goods for re-exportation free of duty, had been in operation for many years in Holland. Indeed, it was the minister's object to narrow his design within the smallest possible compass, and to present its novelty at the lowest. The bill actually introduced to the House of Commons (1733) was simply a proposal to turn the customs duty on the importation of tobacco into an excise duty on its consumption. Instead of paying duty, or giving bonds, on landing the tobacco from Maryland or Virginia on the quays of London or Bristol, the merchant was to lodge his hogsheads in warehouses under the control of excise officers ; to pay duty only as he took it out for home consumption ; and if he took it out, not for the home market, but for re-exportation abroad, then he became free of all payments to the revenue whatever. The same system was to be extended to wine. Various advantages were claimed for the change. First, it would put an end to sundry gross frauds upon the revenue, from smuggling on an immense scale, down to abuses, petty and great, which the ingenuity of dishonest merchants, practising on discounts, allowances, and drawbacks, and the more primitive rapacity of lightermen, watermen, and gangsmen, devised and boldly carried on at every port in the island. Second, the prevention of these frauds and the decrease of smuggling would be a gain to the honest trader. Third, accompanied as it was by a simplification of rates, this cheaper and easier collection would be such an advantage to the revenue as to enable the Chancellor of the Exchequer to please the country gentlemen by taking a shilling off the land tax. Fourth, and much the most important of all, it would tend to make London a free port, and by consequence the market of the world.

It would be ridiculous in the light of modern experience to waste a single line in vindicating the great policy to which Walpole's Tobacco Bill was the opening. The author of the *Wealth of Nations*,[1] writing more than forty years later, had still to lament that none of Walpole's successors had dared to resume a project which in his case factions, politicians, and smuggling merchants successfully resisted. Walpole knew beforehand something of what he had to expect. But though Walpole was cautious and circumspect, he was no craven. He knew that his case was thoroughly sound, and without having any transcendent opinion of human integrity, he had faith in the efficacy of plain reason addressed to solid interests. The Sacheverell episode and the South Sea episode might have taught him the liability of his countrymen to epidemics of unreason, and he was now to see one of these epidemics sweep over them with a violence that shook his power to its foundations.

The bare rumour of his politic design was followed by the fiercest popular outcry that Walpole or any other minister in our history ever encountered. The Opposition espied their chance, and eagerly seized it. A loud note of alarm was raised from one end of the kingdom to the other. The writers of the *Craftsman* brought to bear on a project which was not yet before them, and which they neither understood nor intended to understand, all their powers of wit, misrepresentation, and ingenious calumny. No assertion was too

[1] Bk. v. ch. ii.

wild, no insinuation too incredible, no lie too
glaring. Popular ignorance, prejudice, and passion,
when once thoroughly roused, are never critical,
and any charge was good enough to hurl at " that
plan of arbitrary power, that monster, the excise."
The proposal to put an excise duty on tobacco
and wine became swollen into a general excise.
Food, clothing, and all the other necessaries of life
were to be loaded with a crushing tax. Every
man's house would be invaded at every hour by
the excise officer. Every man's goods and all his
dealings would be exposed to minute and ceaseless
inquisition. A great standing army of revenue
officers would be created, who would overturn
Magna Charta, undermine Parliament, and degrade
Englishmen as low as the wretched slaves on the
other side of the British Channel. The whole
country resounded with shouts of " *No slavery,
no excise, no wooden shoes.*" Are we to sacrifice
the constitution, cried Wyndham, only to prevent
a few frauds on the revenue ? I had rather beg
my bread from door to door, said Sir John Barnard,
and see my country flourish, than be the greatest
subject in the nation and see the trade of my
country decaying, and the people enslaved and
oppressed. Pulteney, with more wit but no less
extravagance, said the minister's fine undertaking
put him in mind of Sir Epicure Mammon in the
Alchemist, who was promised the philosopher's
stone, by which he was to get mountains of gold
and everything that he could desire, but all ended
at last in some little thing for curing the itch.

There were few boroughs that did not despatch
positive directions to their members to oppose
any new excise. The citizens of London, who
might have been expected to resist the frenzy, were
in as great a ferment as people in obscurer places.
They sent a petition with the extraordinary prayer
that they might be heard by counsel against the

new tax, and it was brought by ten citizens in a train of coaches that reached all the way from Westminster to Temple Bar. The beadle and the summoning officer went round every parish in the city, beating up a mob to waylay members at the doors of Parliament. Even the soldiers took it into their heads that the excise would raise the price of their tobacco, and were declared by their generals to be as ripe for mutiny as the nation for rebellion.

The House of Commons kept itself pretty steady. After Walpole had explained and defended his plan, he held his men so well together, considering the vehemence of the cry out of doors, that when the division was taken on the first resolution it was carried by 266 against 205. As the clamour grew more tremendous, the numbers went down at each of the successive stages of the measure, until at length the majority of sixty-one on the main question had on a subsidiary issue sunk to seventeen. From the opening of the session until the middle of April, Walpole stood out the storm. What was quite as important, though no effort was spared to turn them against him, the king and queen held as firm as the minister. Lord Stair sought an audience of the queen and assured her that Walpole was hated by the army as a peaceman, by the clergy as a Whig, by the city because he only regarded the great moneyed companies, and he was hated by the Scotch because he always showed that he hated them. Unluckily, Stair let fall something about his conscience. "Oh, my lord," cried the queen, "don't talk to me of conscience; you will make me faint." She told him that his patriot strain could move her to nothing but laughter; that he only borrowed his politics and his professions from Bolingbroke and Carteret; and that he might, if he thought fit, tell those lords that she had long known them to be two as worthless men of parts as any in this country, and long known them too, both by experience and report, to be two of the greatest liars and knaves in any country.

Walpole expressed his readiness to resign at the very first moment when either the king or the queen should think that such a step would ease their business in Parliament. The queen wondered how he could suppose her to be so mean, cowardly, and ungrateful as to entertain the offer for an instant ; and the king declared that as the minister had done all that could be done for the honour and service of his master, that master would never forsake him ; they would stand or fall together. The king's own best quality was courage, and he admired the same quality in his minister. When Hervey told him of the encounters between Walpole and his enemies in the House of Commons, the king, he says, would often cry out, with colour flushing into his cheeks and tears sometimes in his eyes, and with a vehement oath, " *He is a brave fellow ; he has more spirit than any man I ever knew.*"

The minister, however, was much too wise to suppose that the fidelity of the court was enough to support him against the feeling of the country. He was neither a Strafford nor a North. Nor was he constitutional pedant enough to act as if the mere sanction of a majority in Parliament made a measure either expedient or safe. On the night when his majority had fallen to seventeen, he stood for some time after the House was up, leaning against the table with his hat pulled over his eyes, a few of his friends hanging with melancholy faces around him. He assembled a dozen of them to supper at his house. " *This dance*," he said, " *will no further go.* I meant well, but in the present inflamed temper of the people, the Act could not be carried into execution without an armed force ; and there will be an end of the liberty of England

M

if supplies are to be raised by the sword. If, therefore, the resolution is to proceed with the bill, I will instantly request the king's permission to resign, for I will not be the minister to enforce taxes at the expense of blood."

Accordingly the next day, when the order for the second reading of one of the Tobacco Bills was read, Walpole got up, and in a dexterous speech expressed his intention of postponing it for two months. This was understood to mean the abandonment of the scheme. The Opposition broke out into triumphant jubilation, and the wilder spirits could not restrain the fierceness of their satisfaction. Every night of these debates the Court of Requests, through which members passed on their way to and from the House, had been crowded with an excited throng, who cheered and hooted honourable gentlemen as they were known to have supported or opposed the hated excise. On this last night, when victory might have been expected to make them good-humoured, they were more violent than before, greeting every supporter of the minister with " ironical thanks, hissings, hallooings, and all other insults which it was possible to put upon them without proceeding to blows." Walpole's friends urged him to go out by another way, fearing that his great bulk would make it hard for him to run the gauntlet of the exasperated rioters without being trampled down. He persisted, however, and the tumult was so violent that but for the succour of Pelham and other of his friends he would hardly have escaped with his life.

The abandonment of the bill was the signal for boisterous and universal exultation that lasted for many days. The event was celebrated as if it had been a great victory over Frenchmen or Spaniards. Men went about with badges in their hats, bearing the very foolish inscription, *Liberty,*

Property, and no Excise. The Monument was illuminated. Bonfires were lighted, and the rude mob, so well known to us from the ruthless pencil of Hogarth, flung into the flames with triumphant execrations the effigies of Sir Robert Walpole and a fat woman designed for Queen Caroline. At Oxford the commemoration of victorious folly was spiced with sanguine treason. In that famous home of so many bad causes, for three nights together round the bonfires gownsmen and townsmen drank openly to the good health of Ormond, Bolingbroke, and King James the Third. The last note of the storm was heard more than twenty years later, when Johnson in his dictionary defined excise as " a hateful tax levied upon commodities, and adjudged not by common judges of property, but by wretches hired by those to whom excise is paid."

Walpole did not shrink from making the weight of his resentment felt by some of those who held great posts under the Crown, and yet had ventured to thwart the first minister of the Crown. As Lord Chesterfield was going up the great staircase at St. James's he was summoned by a messenger to the Duke of Grafton, who informed him of the king's command that he should surrender his white staff as Lord Steward. Three other English peers were dismissed from their offices in the household, and three Scotch peers shared the same fate. Even the holders of military commands were as sharply treated as civilians. As a rule, the king strove to retain the affairs of the army in his own hands. If Walpole asked for the smallest commission to oblige a member of Parliament, the king would say, " I won't do it ; you understand nothing of troops ; I will order my army as I think fit ; for your scoundrels of the House of Commons, you may do as you please ; you know I never interfere, or pretend to know anything

of them ; but this province I will keep to myself."
On the great occasion of the excise he allowed
Walpole to have his way.   Two high nobles, Lord
Cobham, the colonel of the king's regiment of
horse, and the Duke of Bolton, colonel of the king's
regiment of guards, were both summarily deprived
of their commands.   Walpole is sometimes blamed
for these high-handed proceedings.   He is accused
of dismissing Chesterfield, for instance, because
Chesterfield had shown the two intolerable qualities
of talent and independence.   Such censure is really
idle.   So far as the civil appointments at any rate
are concerned, Walpole only acted on a principle
which is now part of the accepted foundation of
Cabinet government, and without which nobody
would to-day either form a government or expect
to be a member of a government.   Chesterfield
openly grumbled against the excise bills, and
privately made his brothers vote against them.
He was at the head of the little group of peers who
had long wished Walpole ill in secret, and who
with many meetings, whisperings, and consultations
had persuaded themselves that the hour had come
for striking at him.[1]   It is true that the bills were
dropped, but what minister would have gone on
with a colleague who had helped to force him to
drop them ?   It hardly followed that because
Walpole abandoned the old practice of cutting off
an opponent's head, therefore he was bound to keep
him in a Cabinet.   A weak minister like Pelham
would have overlooked any amount of disloyalty,
but a strong minister like Chatham or Chatham's
son would have acted as Walpole acted.   The
great moralist, we may notice, was on the side of
Thorough.   Dr. Johnson always declared that if
he had been minister he would have done just what
Walpole did.   " If any man wagged his finger at
me, he should be turned out.   If you will not

[1] Hervey, ch. viii.

oppose at the risk of losing your place, your opposition cannot be honest."

Some have argued that Walpole was bound to persist in his scheme or to throw up the seals. It is a surprise to find a writer who united to literary splendour so much practical common sense as Macaulay, blaming Walpole for consenting in deference to popular opinion to abandon a measure which he thought in principle to be right. Peel, with the instinct of the debater, puts a crushing retort into Walpole's mouth ; for Macaulay, though he admitted the corn law to be against principle, had recently (1833) declared himself for maintaining the corn law, simply because the constituencies were divided on the subject. " I at least," Peel makes Walpole reply, " tried the measure which I thought right. I did not abandon it until success was proved to be hopeless and opposition to be universal. But you my accuser, when you are in office, shrink from even the proposal of what you think right. On your own showing you find public opinion not unanimous against your measure, but equally divided as to its merits ; and yet, with all justice and half the people on your side, you do that, without a struggle, which you consider it disgraceful for me to have done after the battle and after defeat." [1]

There is no doubt that Walpole could have carried the excise through Parliament. Only four of his men deserted to the enemy, and most of those who abstained on minor divisions would have come up to the mark on the main question. But the great parliamentary leader knew when it was wise to look beyond the walls of Parliament. It was the difficulty of executing the Act, not of passing the Act, that made him yield. He could have passed it, but he could not carry it out without tumult and disorder. This is in itself a good

[1] Lord Stanhope's *Miscellanies* (1863), p. 80.

answer to the contention that he ought to have resigned. No minister is bound to resign so long as he commands a parliamentary majority, though it may well be held that he is bound to resign or dissolve if he has reason to believe that the majority in Parliament does not represent the constituencies. Sir Robert Peel resigned in the winter of 1845, because he believed that the repeal of the duties on corn had become a pressing necessity, and because he foresaw that he would break up his party if he were to undertake the task. Walpole's circumstances in 1733 were quite different. He knew that his fiscal policy was a wise policy, but it was in no sense a national necessity. He knew that the country could be perfectly well governed without an excise on tobacco, and that to insist on an excise in the face of strong popular opinion would be a piece of exceedingly bad government. Finally, he knew that his resignation would be a grave mischief both to the king and to the country, because it would hand over the public interests to a motley band of ambitious men, partly honest Tories, partly disloyal Jacobites, partly malcontent Whigs, who had no common principles, who had never shown any capacity for common action, and who were now only united by common disappointment and malevolence.

Walpole's handling of the public debt varied with his view of political emergencies, and, like the excise, has exposed him to some censure. When he first came to the Treasury (1717) the national debt stood at fifty-four millions, bearing an average interest of between six and seven per cent. Walpole produced a plan for reducing the interest and establishing a sinking fund for the redemption of the principal.

Ten years later it appeared that the net result of the operation, when taken into account with new debts contracted, was a decrease of the debt by little more than two and a half millions. Walpole professed to adhere to the policy of the sinking fund, and he effected a further reduction of interest from five to four per cent. His virtue, however, did not endure much longer, for after various minor alienations he boldly proposed in 1733 to take half a million from the sinking fund for the service of the year, and he boldly gave the true reasons for this startling attack upon his own provision. He told Parliament that if they would not let him have the money in this way, he should have to raise the land tax from one to two shillings in the pound, and he did not deem it wise thus to increase the burdens that already pressed heavily enough on the landed interest. The sinking fund, " that sacred blessing and the nation's only hope," as some writers called it, was again and again invaded in each subsequent year, so that by the end of 1739, after seventeen years of profound peace, the whole sum paid off was no more than £8,328,000, leaving a capital debt just short of £47,000,000.[1]

If Walpole had been an extravagant minister, and had used for excessive expenditure the funds that might have lightened the load on the next generation, his action would have been without excuse. But no financier was ever more thrifty of the national resources. His motive was political, and in critical times fiscal maxims will always be rightly qualified and governed by political requirements. To bring the Hanoverian Government into favour with the landed men was, as has often been said, one of the cardinal points in Walpole's whole policy and in every part of it. But in laying hands upon the sinking fund, or, in other words, in suspending the payment of debt, he was gratifying two other interests as well. He pleased the fundholders, who did not wish to have their money

[1] See *Wealth of Nations*, bk. v. ch. iii.

thrown on their hands when they had no other
secure investments open. He pleased the general
taxpayer, who is never unwilling to let his masters
shift a burden forward on to the shoulders of future
generations.

The same considerations of general policy explain
Walpole's resistance in 1737 to a proposal made
by Sir John Barnard for reducing the interest on
the national debt to three per cent, and the com-
pulsory redemption of certain annuities existing
at a higher rate. At first Walpole wavered, and
his final decision against the plan was evidently
the result of close observation of public opinion,
and calculation of the strength of the opposing
interests. The whole number of persons affected
by the proposal was 23,000 ; of these, 6000 were
executors or trustees for widows and orphans,
and more than 17,000 were proprietors of sums
not exceeding one thousand pounds. To this large
class the reduction of their income by one-fourth
would be a serious distress and embarrassment.
The minister had a stronger reason for not wounding
the moneyed interest. He foresaw the too probable
approach of an early war with Spain, and he knew
how great would be the advantage in that emergency of having the men with money to lend in
a good humour, and of keeping the public faith
with the creditors even more punctiliously than
strict legality required.

Even those who blame Walpole for what they
regard as a selfish and timid sacrifice of the real
interests of the country to personal convenience,
admit that the public debt might be viewed as a
pillar of the Hanoverian government. The notion
that the Pretender, if he came into his own again,
would repudiate a debt contracted to keep him
out of his own, obviously made every fundholder
a zealous partisan of the existing establishment.
It was in vain that Jacobites protested that the

Spectator's vision of James with a flaming sword in one hand and a sponge in the other, was a vile Whig calumny.[1] The public creditor pinned his faith on Walpole, and Walpole took care that he should have good grounds for his faith. For many years the public conviction was as strong as that of George I., that Walpole could make gold from nothing, and anticipated the later judgment of economic writers that Walpole was the greatest commercial minister that this country had then ever seen.

[1] See Lord Stanhope's *History of England*, ch. xvi. p. 158, 5th ed.

CHAPTER IX

FOREIGN historians sometimes talk of the torpor of the Walpolean era. Doubtless the era had none of the glory of Elizabeth, or Cromwell, or Chatham. Yet it was now that the bearers of two of the most illustrious names in the literary history of the century came to kindle in England the lamp of European illumination. Voltaire visited this country in 1726, and Montesquieu followed him hither in 1732. It was Walpole's England that inspired the *Philosophic Letters* and the *Spirit of Laws*. The violence of faction, the froth of parliamentary passion, the boisterous humours of elections, did not divert these brilliant and sincere observers from the truth of the matter. They felt the movement, the freedom, the full pulse and current of vitality, under an uninteresting surface. The fact that Voltaire deemed most worthy of attention under the head of government was equality of taxation. The contrast between England and France was a poignant one to his humane and social intelligence. " Here," he said, " the peasant has not his feet bruised by sabots, he eats white bread, he is well clad, he is not afraid of increasing the number of his cattle or putting tiles on his house, lest next year he should have his taxes raised." He noticed with amazement and admiration that in England the younger son of a peer did not disdain to carry on useful business in the city, while in France he would have scorned any life outside the frivolous slavery of Versailles. Though the government was in the hands of an aristocratic oligarchy, the oligarchy was not a caste. Later economists believe that the earnings of the labourer have not for many ages commanded so large a portion of subsistence as at this period of the eighteenth century. Hallam, like Malthus, is of opinion that, in respect of the real happiness of the community, the reign of George II. might be advantageously compared with the more brilliant but less steady condition of later times.[1]

One of the grand articles against Walpole is, that though he was at the head of affairs for so many years, not one great measure, not one important change for better or worse, marks the period of his supremacy. He ought, according to Whigs of our day, to have shortened the duration of Parliaments ; yet all the wisest of the reforming Whigs of that and the next generation held that more frequent elections would be an aggravation of every parliamentary mischief. He ought to have insisted on limiting the number of placemen and excluding pensioners ; yet when the innovators set to work in 1780 they judiciously sought for a real remedy, not in the exclusion of placemen, but the suppression of places. The patriots who had clamoured against Walpole's corruption for twenty years, tolerated, practised, and aggravated every evil of his system for twenty years after.

Before they blame Walpole for not introducing great measures and making important changes, his critics ought to say for what important change the time was ripe and the opportunity safe. A vast and important change had been made at the accession of the Hanoverian line. The one object of a wise minister was not to make other changes, but to guard that. Some ministers are great

[1] *Constitutional History*, ch. xvi. 8, 302, 10th ed.

because they pass great bills, others because they either prepare or secure them. Walpole was a great minister of the second of these two orders. Why should we mete out to him a measure which nobody applies to other statesmen of his commanding position ? Walpole has rather a bad character and the younger Pitt has an exceedingly good one : so Walpole is condemned as selfish and unprincipled for not being a reformer and not helping the dissenters, while Mr. Pitt stands undisturbed on his pedestal, though he spoke against meddling with the Test Act, though he allowed parliamentary reform, which he had taken up in Opposition, to drop when he was in power, and though he solemnly abandoned Catholic emancipation after as solemnly treating it as a condition of a great international compact. In saying this, I am not judging Pitt, but offering a standard by which we may judge Walpole.

Political tranquillity was a condition of material advance. Under the appearance of torpor, men were minding their business, and preparing the ways and means for that immense expansion which we associate with the name and policy of Chatham. Taxes were light ; public credit was high ; the administration of justice, which after taxation is the most important branch of government for the happiness of a people, was, on the whole, upright, equal, and sure. Even in the spiritual sphere, historians of thought have been justified in asking whether in the first half of the nineteenth century we could find three bishops of higher purity and devotion than Berkeley, Butler, and Wilson ; divines more honest and manly than Clarke, or with a finer glow of devout sentiment than Law ; workers of more honourable and laborious life than Watts, Lardner, and Doddridge, who all of them sacrificed preferment to conscience.[1]

[1] See Sir Leslie Stephen's *English Thought in the Eighteenth Century*, ii. 384.

The dissenters, it is true, still laboured under disabilities. The Acts against occasional conformity and in restraint of the rights of dissenters to educate their children had been repealed in 1719 (*ante*, p. 50). A motion for the repeal of the Test Act was thrown out in 1736 by Walpole's advice. As the dissenters were peaceful and law-abiding, and gave him no trouble, he would run no risk for their sake, and Sacheverell had taught him how sharp and serious the risk might be. All this is true enough, but it would have been little less than madness in any statesman, for a generation at least, to forget for a day the lesson of the Sacheverell explosion. That extraordinary outbreak had led to the Tory government of the last four years of Queen Anne, and —to use again a strong expression that I have borrowed before—nothing short of the greatest miracle in our history prevented the Tory government of the last four years of Anne ending in either a legitimist restoration or a civil war. A statesman who had seen the constitution come so close as that to disaster, might well think it better that the dissenters should continue for some time longer to endure harsh laws, than that new provocation to the Church should bring back old peril to the State.

Three years later the dissenters again approached Walpole, urging the repeal of the Test Act. He gave them the reply, so well known from all ministers to all reformers, that he quite agreed with them, but that the time was not opportune. One of the deputation hardily asked him when the time would come. " If you want a specific answer," said Walpole, " I will give it you in a single word—Never." But reparation was made by the Indemnity Act, first passed in the first year of George II., and renewed every year afterwards with three or four interruptions down to 1828, when the sacramental test disappeared. The test remained, to please the pride of Churchmen, but if a dissenter chose to break it with certain not unimportant limitations, he could evade the penalty. The struggle against occasional conformity had been inspired, not merely by dislike of religious toleration, but by the solid political object of closing to dissenters the corporations which returned members of Parliament. Walpole's policy as to tests secured the practical victory, while leaving the obnoxious flag of church privilege still flying. Lord Chancellor Cowper informed George I. on his accession that, if the clergy could be brought round, all differences of opinion as to the royal title would soon vanish among the laity. This extraordinary and dangerous authority would undoubtedly have been exerted against the parliamentary constitution, as the authority of clericalism has been in France, if Walpole had roused latent passions. The closing of the doors of Convocation in 1717 was an effective protest against the virulence of ecclesiastical controversy, and no other was ever demanded.

Early in his career, Walpole had encountered the obduracy of Scottish sentiment. In 1725 the disgust of the English country gentlemen at the exemption of Scotland from the duty on malt, had grown so clamorous as to force him to propose a sixpenny tax on every barrel of ale brewed in Great Britain. The Scots took fire. All the dialectic ingenuity of the race was invoked against the obnoxious sixpence. The transfer of the duty on malt to a duty on beer was contrary to the Act of Union : now the violation of any material article of a compact is a legal dissolution of the whole : therefore the Union was dissolved. But the dissolution of the Union revived the Scottish Act of 1681. Therefore King George was no longer entitled to Scottish allegiance, and the next in

succession of the Stuart line became King of
Scotland. This train of argument was decorated
with references to the separation of Denmark
from Sweden, to the rejection of the yoke of Spain
by the United Provinces, and to the revolt of
Israel from Judah. The Scots had resisted the
oppressions of Charles II. and James VII. : should
they not now resist the tyrannical minister who
had riveted chains upon his king and his country ?

Violent tumults broke out in Glasgow and other
towns. The troops were called out, and there
was considerable loss of life. The Edinburgh
brewers entered into a solemn compact that they
would rather not brew than pay the duty. The
government held firm. Proceedings were instituted
against the brewers for payment of the duty on
stock in hand. They were told that nothing would
be listened to, short of entire submission. They
met to discuss the question, *Brew or not brew?*
The chairman began to take the votes on his
right hand ; but the right-hand man thought it
hard upon him to have to speak first, and the left-
hand man thought the same, and nobody would
be the first to speak. At length one man plucked
up courage to vote *Brew*, and by noon the next
day, says Walpole, forty brewhouses were hard
at work in Edinburgh and ten more in Leith.
This satisfactory result was due to the firmness and judgment of Lord Islay. The Duke of
Roxburghe, then Secretary of State for Scotland
and a friend of Carteret, had secretly encouraged
resistance by representations that the days of
Walpole's power were numbered. The minister
sent prompt remonstrances to the king, and Roxburghe was compelled to resign.

The circumstances of the Porteous riot are
familiar wherever the English tongue is spoken,
because they were made the dramatic opening of
one of his finest stories by that admirable genius

who, like Shakespeare in his plays, has conveyed
to plain men more of the spirit and action of the
past in noble fiction, than they would find in most
professed chronicles of fact. The early scenes of
The Heart of Midlothian are an accurate account
of the transaction which gave so much trouble to
Queen Caroline and the minister. A smuggler
who had excited the popular imagination by his
daring and his chivalry was sentenced to be hanged ;
after his execution the mob pressed forward to
cut down his body : Porteous, the captain of the
City Guard, ordered his men to fire, and several
persons were shot dead : he was tried for murder,
convicted, and sentenced, but at the last moment
a reprieve arrived from London, to the intense
indignation of a crowd athirst for vengeance :
four days later, under mysterious ringleaders who
could never afterwards be discovered, fierce throngs
suddenly gathered together at nightfall to the
beat of drum, broke into the prison, dragged out
the unhappy Porteous, and sternly hanged him
on a dyer's pole close by the common place of
public execution.

Carteret thought that these wild doings furnished
good material for a parliamentary attack (1737).
If the government did nothing, he could denounce
them for indifference to law and order. If they
took sharp measures, he knew that it would
kindle the resentment of the Scotch. In either
case, moreover, he would discredit the authority of
Lord Islay, to whom the minister looked for the
management of Scotch affairs. This calculation
proved quite correct. Walpole was bound to cover
Lord Islay, as well as his brother the Duke of
Argyll, and he dreaded lest the affair should
become national. The Lord Provost of Edinburgh
and four bailies were summoned to the bar of the
House of Lords, and it at once became evident
that so far as feeling in Scotland went, the affair

was already national in its full extent. Their testimony showed that ninety-nine Scotchmen out of every hundred thought that Porteous had been justly condemned, and justly put to death. Islay warned Walpole that any attempt to inflict excessive punishment for Porteous's murder, would make the whole of Scotland disaffected, and would render the government of the country impossible.

In the course of a prolonged and acrimonious controversy the Scottish judges were examined at the bar of the House of Lords ; and a bill of pains and penalties was brought in for disqualifying the Provost of Edinburgh for all magisterial office in Great Britain ; inflicting on him a term of imprisonment ; abolishing the Town Guard of the city ; and removing the gates of the Nether Bow Port. This stringent bill passed the House of Lords by a majority of fifty-four to twenty-two. On reaching the Commons it immediately encountered very rude treatment. The forty-five Scottish members, regarding the bill as an insult to their nation, were against it to a man. The Tories professed to be opposed on principle to all bills of pains and penalties. Things began to look as if the bill would be flung out, and all Walpole's tact was required to prevent a parliamentary disaster. After a heated conflict the imprisonment of the Provost was dropped, and so were the clauses for disbanding the Town Guard and demolishing the town gate. In their stead a provision was inserted, imposing a fine of two thousand pounds on the Corporation for the benefit of Porteous's widow. The generality of mankind, says Hervey, looking on these great transactions in cold blood, were not a little amused at Parliament spending five months in declaring that a man should never again be a magistrate who had never wished to be one, and in raising two thousand pounds on the city of Edinburgh, to make the widow of Captain Porteous with

N

unconjugal joy bless the hour in which her husband was hanged.

The course of these affairs contains the best answer to the charge, made by Macaulay among others, that it was the obvious and pressing duty of a British statesman to break the power of the Highland chiefs, and that it was through Walpole's failure to regulate the Highlands in a time of peace, that his successors were forced to conquer them in the middle of a war with France and Spain. In 1738 Duncan Forbes, the acute and well-informed President of the Court of Session, submitted a scheme for raising four or five thousand men in the Highlands ; the disaffected districts would thus be drained ; the pride of the chiefs would be gratified by the bestowal of his Majesty's commission ; and active military life would please the martial tastes of the clansmen. Walpole saw what was to be gained, and approved generally of the scheme.[1] Two considerations of different degrees of weight made him hesitate. One was the clamour, always very loud, and just then particularly likely to rise to its stormiest pitch, against a standing army. The other and stronger argument was the intense national sentiment of Scotland, so vividly shown in the recent affair of Porteous, and the certainty that the levy of a large Highland force by order of the government would undoubtedly have been represented as a design on the national freedom. On these grounds, we hold that Walpole was right in leaving the Highlands alone. What was easy for Pitt, after all fear of the Stuarts had practically come to an end, and after the spirit of partisanship and intrigue had died out of the Highlands, even if it was not actually impossible in Walpole's time, would without dispute have been extremely dangerous.

The resentment of Scotland could not make

[1] *The Culloden Papers*, p. xxxi.

itself felt before the arrival of a general election, which was still four years off. Meanwhile Walpole was suddenly confronted with formidable and pressing peril nearer home. The smouldering hatred within the royal family burst out in a fierce explosion in 1737. Walpole described this unnatural conflict as the most troublesome and the most dangerous he had yet known. It arose from the marriage of the Prince of Wales, and was destined to have in the fulness of time a disastrous effect on the fortunes of Walpole. Prince Frederick, like his grandson George IV., is a striking instance of the common and inevitable contrast in courts between important position and paltry character. By placing himself at the head of the able band in opposition, he took the sting out of Walpole's standing charge, that the coalition was essentially Jacobite ; and the adhesion of the heir to the throne marked a signal change in the position of Pulteney, Wyndham, Carteret, and their friends. The prince was vain, childish, and truthless. In 1745, when the news arrived that the Highland rebels had reached Derby, and that his brother had marched northward to meet them, he was found playing at blindman's buff with the pages. He had a passion for disguising himself and running off to bull-baits at Hockley-in-the-Hole. He was incontinent of speech, heedless of all correspondence between words and things, and while overflowing with conceit, was destitute of self-respect. This was the material out of which Bolingbroke designed to make his first Patriot King.

The prince, on his marriage, found his allowance of £50,000 not enough for his new establishment. It was, moreover, intensely galling to him to feel that even this sum was not permanently settled by the arrangement of Parliament, but took the form of an annual gratuity from his father. To have too little money was bad enough, but to owe even a meagre

income to the good-will of a man whom he hated,
was unbearable. Bolingbroke and Chesterfield were
at his ear, with the sinister counsel that he should
bring his irksome situation to an end by boldly
laying his case before Parliament. If Parliament
could be induced to request the king to settle
£100,000 a year on the prince, with a jointure on
the princess, then he would have gained three grand
objects : he would have acquired a proper income,
secured his own emancipation, and mortally vexed
his father. The news that the prince had fallen in
with this suggestion, exasperated the court beyond
all control. The queen a hundred times a day
cursed the hour in which her eldest son had been
born, and a hundred times a day she and the Princess
Caroline wished that he might drop down dead of
an apoplexy. The angry fires did not burn any the
less furiously from the apprehension that the prince
might carry Parliament with him. Lists made out
by his own friends promised him a majority of forty,
and even the minister's list could not bring it lower
than ten. Walpole took serious alarm. He saw
that the moderate people, on whom he always relied,
felt the injustice of leaving the princess without a
jointure, and the prince a pensioner at pleasure on
the king. Accordingly, with much difficulty, he
persuaded the king to send his son a message,
promising a jointure and a settled allowance of
£50,000. He knew the risk he ran, in the inflamed
state of mind of his royal masters, of rousing the
shadow of a suspicion that he was currying favour
with the prince. " But it is my way, you know," he
said to Hervey, " and when you come to be in my
place, I advise you to make it your way too, to provide against the present difficulty that presses." He
could make the best of the royal jealousies another
day. Meanwhile, the prince shuffled, begged the
ministers who conveyed the message to him to lay
him at his Majesty's feet, to assure his Majesty of

his utmost duty for the royal person, and of his sense of the royal goodness and graciousness ; but that the affair was now out of his hands, and he could give no answer.

The king was more enraged than ever, and roughly reproached Walpole for subjecting him to such a repulse. Walpole answered that the good he expected from the proceeding was to be reaped to-morrow, not to-day ; and that what he had proposed by it was to bring the House of Commons to reason, not the Prince of Wales. When Pulteney brought on the motion for an address begging the king to settle £100,000 a year on the heir-apparent, Walpole replied in a speech of singular firmness and address. After a long debate, the motion was lost by a handsome majority of thirty against it. It was commonly supposed to have cost the court a great deal of money in bribing members of Parliament, and the king, though delighted with the result, grumbled at the amount. Yet it appears that the cost, after all, did not exceed £900, in two sums of £500 and £400 respectively, to two gentlemen who were to have received the money at the end of the session in any case, and who only took advantage of this particular occasion to exact prompt payment. This is the one definite case of direct parliamentary bribery in Walpole's history.

" If ever any man in any cause," said Walpole afterwards, " fought dagger out of sheath, I did so in the House of Commons that day." He knew that he carried his political life in his hand. If he leaned ever so slightly towards the prince, he ruined himself with the king and queen. If he defied the prince, he ruined himself with the man who might be king to-morrow. The king, as it happened, had barely recovered from a serious illness, and to people in the lively and morbid expectancy that is natural to all Oppositions, it seemed that he might disappear any day. Bolingbroke expressed his amazement at

Walpole's imprudence.　In truth Walpole knew very
well what he was about.　He acted on the maxims
which had been the key to his success.　He had
recognised what was just in the prince's demand.
By conceding it he had put his opponents in the
wrong.　He averted the actual and present difficulty with the king, without regard to the con-
tingency of future difficulties with the prince.
When we hear of the mischief of a system which
makes great ministers responsible to the public
opinion of democracy, it is well to remember
the embarrassments and dangers that beset great
ministers from the private passions of a court.

The miscarriage of the project that was to have
done such fine things for him, made it all the more
odious to the prince to have to live under the same
roof with his detested parents at Hampton Court
or at St. James's.　He attended drawing-rooms and
levees, and dined with the court in public ; but the
queen, though she allowed him to take her hand,
never spoke to him, and the king pretended to be
wholly unconscious of his presence.　The prince
suddenly brought things to a violent crisis.　One
night (1737), while the royal family were at Hampton
Court, the princess was seized with the pains of
labour.　She was hurried into a chaise and driven
off at the risk of her life at full gallop to St. James's,
where in less than an hour after her arrival, the
unfortunate lady was delivered.　The queen was
roused at one in the morning with the news of the
flight ;　she instantly dressed, ordered coaches,
hurried after the singular fugitives, and by four
found herself at St. James's at the bedside of her
daughter-in-law.　The king's fury at his son's
escapade knew no bounds.　Scoundrel and puppy,
knave and fool, liar and coward, were on his lips at
every moment.　It was all Walpole's fault, for
forcing his master to settle £50,000 a year on the
ingrate, and so make him independent for life.

Walpole took the royal storm with his usual composure. At the same time he knew very well that the feud between the king and the prince was also a struggle between himself and the Opposition. The prince was nothing without Carteret and Pulteney, Bolingbroke and Chesterfield. Some of his own colleagues, too, were less intrepid than himself. They were less disposed than he was to burn their boats, to cut off all hopes of future honour and emolument, and Lord Hardwicke especially remonstrated against the asperity of the message by which the king turned his son out of doors. This only made Walpole more determined to hold to his own course against prince, Opposition, and trimming colleagues. The Chancellor, the Duke of Newcastle, and others who were of the same mind, were for giving the prince another chance of making his submission. No, said Walpole, there is nothing like taking it " short at first." The prince was ordered instantly to quit St. James's Palace, and he borrowed the Duke of Norfolk's house in St. James's Square. The guard was taken away from his door. There was even an ignoble squabble as to the articles of furniture which he had a right to carry with him. The foreign ministers were informed that it would be agreeable to the king if they abstained from visiting the prince. A written message was even sent to all peers, peeresses, and Privy Councillors, that if they went to the prince's court they would be excluded from the king's presence. The prince was not to wait many years for revenge. As we shall see, when the critical moment arrived, he became the principal agent in depriving the king of his minister, and driving Walpole from power.

The heaviest blow in Walpole's ministerial career followed these vexatious events. In the winter of 1737 Queen Caroline died. From an excess of delicacy remarkable in one of her strong character, and only to be accounted for by the peculiar nature

of her relations with her husband, she concealed
from her physicians an infirmity with which she
had for some years been afflicted. They pursued
an erroneous course of treatment, and when they
discovered her secret it was too late. She met her
end with serenity and fortitude. One unnatural
antipathy burnt fiercely to the close ; the clergy
made her profess forgiveness of her eldest son, but
to the last she refused to see him. The king hovered
incessantly about her bedside, sometimes blubber-
ing and maudlin, sometimes bullying and peevish.
No more extraordinary death-bed conversation can
ever have taken place between husband and wife.
The dying queen urged him to marry again. Wiping
his eyes, and his voice choked by sobs, he ejaculated,
" *Non, j'aurai des maîtresses.*"—" *Ah, mon Dieu !* "
replied the queen, " *cela n'empêche pas.*" When
Walpole arrived the king took him to the bedside.
The queen said, "My good Sir Robert, you see me
in a very indifferent situation. I have nothing to
say to you, but to recommend the king, and my
children, and the kingdom to your care."

The change in Walpole's position was profound,
and everybody was sensible of it and acted upon it.
" Though he may have more power with the king
than any other body," said the shrewd Chesterfield,
" yet he will never have that kind of power which
he had by her means, and he will never dare to
mention many things to the king, which he would
without difficulty have brought about by her
means." [1] Newcastle and the Chancellor were even
emboldened to talk to the king on their own
account. The difficulty of managing the House of
Commons was increased by the rise in the demands
of his followers of the baser sort, in proportion to
his greater need for them. The resentment of the
heir to the throne for the affronts that Walpole had
put upon him, became keener as he saw a nearer

[1] 12th November 1787, v. 427.

chance of gratifying it. All this only brings into stronger relief the bluff courage with which Walpole, now left standing absolutely alone, confronted the fury of Opposition, the selfishness of colleagues, and the sudden humours of the king.

CHAPTER X

FOREIGN POLICY

IT is a misfortune for the popularity of Walpole's reputation that the most important chapter in his policy should have become in its details the least interesting. Even the vivid genius of Carlyle could not bring to life again the European diplomacy of the eighteenth century. Congresses without issue, campaigns without visible objective, open treaties, secret articles, public alliances, private combinations, the destruction to-day of the web laboriously woven yesterday, the union of four powers against one, of three against two, and so on in every possible variety of permutation and combination, make a vast chaos in comparison with which even the perturbed Europe of to-day is a scene of stability and order. Towards the close of Walpole's rule momentous issues for Great Britain and for mankind arose on the blurred horizon of continental struggles in diplomacy and the field. Until that time Walpole's guiding principle was to hold England back from European strife.

Peace was indispensable to the success of his policy. It was essential alike to material development and political consolidation. War meant high expenditure and a land tax at four shillings, whereas he sought to reconcile the landed men to the new settlement by keeping the land tax low. War was an interruption of that energetic devotion to trade and manufacture which was so remarkable a sign

of the time, and which was every year adding
enormously to the wealth and strength of the
country. In case of war our enemy would assuredly
launch the Pretender and rouse the Jacobites, if
not in England, at any rate in Scotland. War, in
fine, would certainly at an earlier or later stage
come to be associated in the public mind with the
Hanoverian connection, and the burdens of war
would become so many arguments against the
dynasty. For all these cogent reasons, peace has
never been so imperative an object to Great Britain
as it was for the generation after Utrecht.

Townshend advanced a certain way in the path
of non-intervention, but not on principle or system.
To Walpole belongs the chief credit of perceiving
that the time had come for altering the foreign
policy of his party. The Whigs had supported King
William in his vast schemes of continental alliances
and campaigns. Year after year they had placed
all the resources of England at the disposal of
Marlborough. They had denounced and resisted
the Peace of Utrecht, and with every circumstance
of passion and animosity had impeached its authors.
With Walpole new maxims definitely arose within
the Whig party. Principles of peace, of neutrality,
of diplomacy as a substitute for war, began slowly
to find favour among them. Walpole did not carry
the whole of the party with him in his new departure; and if here were the proper place it would
be interesting to trace this great line of division
between the two sections of Whigs down to the end
of the century; to show how the differences between
Walpole and Sunderland were reproduced between
Walpole and Carteret; how the tradition of the
Sunderland Whigs was carried on by the elder Pitt,
and from him descended to Shelburne; how it
was opposed by Burke and the Rockingham Whigs
— the representatives of Walpole's policy with
loftier phrases and a deeper morality—how it helps

to explain the quarrels between Shelburne and Fox ;
how the younger Pitt, who so long looked on himself
as a Whig, acted mainly on Walpolean maxims, until
Burke flung them over under the stress of the French
Revolution and compelled Pitt to do the same.

At the beginning of this great change in the policy
of his party, neither Walpole nor any other minister
could have carried it forward to a logical end.
Absolute non-intervention was impracticable. The
king's Hanoverian dominions involved us in Germany, as well as in the affairs of both Russia and
Sweden in the north. The retention of Gibraltar
involved us for many years with Spain. Our
commerce with Spanish dependencies was the most
extensive branch of British trade. The emperor's
diplomacy was expressly directed against our commercial marine. Finally, we were still under the
general obligations of Utrecht. British interests in
European affairs were therefore direct, active, and
substantial.

On the other side, in estimating the state of
Europe, the minister saw the continent distracted
by the plots and counterplots of ambitious and unscrupulous rulers at Vienna and Madrid. He saw
Russia beginning to use her new ascendancy in the
north against the declining power of Sweden and
Denmark. Holland was slowly losing, and Prussia
was surely gaining, a position of decisive prominence.
Hardly a pretence of public right guarded the state
system of Europe. What Queen Caroline wittily
observed of the Triple Alliance of 1735, was equally
true of the other combinations of the age. It
always put her in mind, she said, of the South Sea
scheme; people went into it knowing that it was
all a cheat, still hoping to get something out of
it; everybody meaning when he had made his own
fortune to be the first in scrambling away, and each
thinking himself sharp enough to be able to leave
his fellow-adventurers in the lurch.

When George I. in 1723 requested Walpole to
provide funds for operations against the Czar in his
attempt to depose the King of Sweden, the minister
found the money, but hoped that it might never be
wanted. " *My politics*," he said, " *are to keep free
from all engagements as long as we possibly can.*"
Engagements were inevitable. No wide and comprehensive settlement of Europe was possible. For
us no standing system of foreign policy was possible.
It was an epoch of transition ; too late to found a
European policy on religion, too early to found it
on nationality ; the dynastic struggle which had
raged for so many years was coming to an end ; the
struggle for trade and the New World was beginning.
It was no time for ambitious general views, and
Walpole was not the man to bewilder himself, either
by fictitious contingencies or by any of the wild
schemes that fascinated the rash and erratic genius
of Carteret. It would be absurd to ascribe to him
any of those great ideals of European peace which
had inspired men in the fourteenth century, and
were soon in new forms to revive in the superior
speculative minds of the eighteenth. The first
and most remarkable of these modern schemes of
universal peace had been suggested to the fertile
and benevolent intelligence of the abbé Saint-Pierre
by his experience at Utrecht ; but Walpole was not
the man to be interested by utopian speculation.
He had none of those high dreams of the universal
mediator and peacemaker which men had hoped to
realise first in the Papacy, and then in the Holy
Roman Empire, and which was now in the second
of these august institutions so terribly miscarrying.
Walpole was a man not of ideals, but of expedients,
as the commander of an army in a campaign is a
man of expedients. He looked at each crisis as it
arose, from the point of the actual, positive, direct,
and particular interests of England ; and the one
general view that he permitted himself was the wise

and noble one that England's best interest lay in European peace.

The only hope for European peace lay in an alliance between England and France. Circumstances for the time made these two powers the mediators and peacemakers of Europe. The policy of Wolsey, of Elizabeth when she acted with Henry IV., of Cromwell when he acted with Mazarin, was reproduced by Walpole's alliance with Cardinal Fleury. Walpole probably did not very well know, and certainly did not at all care, what had been done by Wolsey, Elizabeth, or Cromwell ; but he renewed their tradition, and by union with France, from his first entry into real power down to the second Treaty of Vienna in 1731, he secured for Europe intervals of peace in a period of extraordinary confusion and danger. The co-operation with Fleury was not always equally close, its aspect varied with the passing circumstances, it was always guarded, qualified, cautious, suspicious, it was often informal and unsystematic, occasionally it gave way ; but it was strong enough and persistent enough to produce a certain amount of rough and practical peace, and it presents one of the most remarkable, satisfactory, and instructive pictures in the modern history of Europe.[1] Here again Walpole departed from the old tradition of his own party. It was enough to make King William's Whigs turn in their grave, that the influence of George I. should have procured a cardinal's hat for a prime minister of France ; that the British ambassador should be concerting military plans at Versailles with Marshal Berwick, the son of King James ; and that a serious proposal should come to King George to allow his eldest daughter to turn Catholic and marry Louis XV.

Between 1725 and 1731 the positions of Spain and

---

[1] For the French view of Walpole's influence over Fleury, see St-Simon, xv. 325 (ed. 1874).

the Empire underwent incessant change. The congress of Cambrai had long been sitting under the auspices of Great Britain and France as mediators, to compose the differences arising out of their rivalry. Europe was suddenly informed that the rivals had composed their own differences and made the Treaty of Vienna (1725). The emperor, Spain, and Russia drew themselves up in line against the rest of Europe. England's direct concern lay in certain secret articles that were alleged to exist, by which Spain was to be supported in attacking Gibraltar, the emperor to be supported in the Ostend Company and his other maritime and commercial designs, and the Pretender to be supported by the Empire, Spain, and Russia. The immediate retort to the Treaty of Vienna was the Treaty of Hanover (September 1725) between England, France, and Prussia. This combination was for many years bitterly attacked by the pamphleteers and orators of the Opposition. The very name of the treaty enabled them to represent it as a sacrifice of England to the German electorate. It was in truth to expose the electorate for the sake of England. Walpole himself, though he defended the Treaty of Hanover in Parliament, doubted whether Townshend's apprehensions were not exaggerated, and, looking to the quarter in which it was his characteristic habit to look, he doubted whether the House of Commons would willingly grant the subsidies. The despatch of a squadron to the Baltic convinced Russia that the new allies were in earnest, and it arrested mischief in the north. In the south Spain opened the siege of Gibraltar, the emperor got his forces together, Prussia fell away from the allies of Hanover, and a general conflagration became imminent. Only the prudence of Walpole and the good faith of Fleury prevented it. A British expedition was sent to the Spanish West Indies, but the admiral had instructions not to act on the offensive. The allies were ready to assist us against the Spanish attack, but Walpole insisted on delay, and begged them to wait. We may almost wonder even in our own enlightened day, how a minister could dare to be so sensible as Walpole. Though this resolute tardiness in recourse to arms exposed him to taunts of pusillanimity then and since, he was speedily justified by the event. Within a few months the emperor, finding himself without any of the outside support on which he had reckoned, withdrew from his engagements with Spain, the Treaty of Vienna fell to pieces, and, as a result of the mediation of France, the preliminaries of peace were signed by the emperor with England, France, and Holland (1727). The death of George I. and the hopes which that event, and the expected fall of Walpole as a consequence, inspired in the enemies of England, caused some delay in ratifying the preliminaries, and it was not until after a period of dangerous suspense that in the spring of 1729 Great Britain, France, and Spain executed the Treaty of Seville. To England various commercial rights were restored which had been invaded by the Treaty of Vienna in 1725. Gibraltar was not mentioned. The charter of the Ostend Company was to be suspended. Spain was to be allowed under guarantees to introduce a force into Tuscany and Parma, as a security that the succession in these two provinces should revert to Don Carlos. The Treaty of Seville thus made a useful peace in one quarter, but, so complex and intricate was the game, it was a provocation to war in another. It left the emperor isolated and resentful, disappointed alike in his dynastic schemes and in his imperial claims. Walpole, who was now free by the resignation of Townshend to pursue his own views, immediately addressed himself to Vienna. Without consulting Fleury, he proposed to the emperor to guarantee the succession of his daughter to the hereditary dominions of the House of Hapsburg in return for the abolition of the Ostend Company, and for the imperial assent to the entry of the Spanish troops into Parma. The emperor, to whom the succession of Maria Theresa had long been the main object of his life, came in to these terms, and after some difficulties in connection with the electorate of Hanover had been boldly thrust aside by Walpole for future arrangement, his grand plan was finally accepted in the second Treaty of Vienna in 1731. The European explosion was once more postponed.

None of these arduous transactions show Walpole's difficulties more instructively than those which arose out of the vacancy of the crown of Poland in 1733. The events themselves are dead, but they show Walpole's method at its best. His ends were wise, his diplomatic management was penetrating and skilful, and his union of tact and patience with immovable determination is a standing lesson in political action. On the death of the King of Poland a violent struggle instantly began for the choice of a successor. France supported Stanislaus, the father of the French king's consort, already once the wearer of the uneasy Polish crown. The emperor favoured Augustus, the Elector of Saxony, and son of the late king. Russia took sides with Austria, and Spain joined France. Stanislaus suddenly appeared in the midst of the turbulent nobles, and was hailed king by acclamation; Russia at once sent an armed force into Warsaw. Stanislaus took to flight, and the partisans of Augustus elected him in triumph. France, Spain, and Sardinia immediately declared war against the emperor as instigator of the Russian attack. By the beginning of 1734 Spain had made herself mistress of his possessions in southern Italy, Russia was of little avail, and in his straits he addressed importunate appeals to England. The

success of the operations against the emperor had
raised wider issues than the difference between a
French and an Austrian nominee on the Polish
throne. Was Great Britain to see her ancient ally
beaten and stripped by England's ancient enemies,
French and Spanish Bourbons ? Was there not
good ground to suspect a Family Compact ? Was
Great Britain to watch with indifference such a
derangement of the balance of power in Europe as
must inevitably follow, if the war went on and the
emperor were left to his fate ? George II. answered
questions of this kind by vehement declarations
in favour of succouring the emperor. He was a
German and hated the French. As Elector of
Hanover he was part and member of the Empire,
and bound to its head. His martial passion always
flamed out at the prospect of war. The emperor
offered his vanity an almost irresistible temptation
by actually proposing to place him in command of
the imperial army on the Rhine.

The queen's German sympathies drew her
towards the same views. Most of the Cabinet
were with the king. Newcastle used as big words
as his master about driving the Spaniards out
of Italy and humbling the pride of France. Lord
Grantham reiterated his policy in the simple
creed, " I hate the French, and I hope as we shall
beat the French." [1] Lord Harrington, the Secretary
of State in whose department the most important
part of the negotiation was officially conducted,
leaned strongly for war. The Opposition raised
the familiar cry for national honour and fidelity
to our allies. The emperor sent envoy after envoy
to intrigue for Walpole's overthrow. Fleury, with
a council of state full of marshals, had difficulties
of his own, and he more than once betrayed the
British minister by shifts, tricks, evasions, and
downright lying. Walpole for a long time stood

[1] Hervey, ii. 42.

entirely alone. He held out resolutely against
armed intervention. " Madam," he said compla-
cently to the queen one morning (1734), " there
are fifty thousand men slain this year in Europe,
and not one Englishman." He kept his hand firm
on the helm, scanning every shift of wind and
current at Vienna, Madrid, Versailles, the Hague,
and making a series of tacks so skilful and so
effectual that even at this distance of time it is
impossible for a political reader not to follow them
with some of the lively interest that is commonly
reserved for our own affairs.

He read all the despatches that arrived or were
sent ; he carried on an unwearied private correspondence of his own with his brother and other
agents at the continental courts ; and he personally
directed the whole of a long course of negotiations,
as intricate and as delicate as any European statesman ever meddled with. It is important to remark
that though Walpole was firmly decided that not
an Englishman should be killed either to support
Augustus in Poland, or to recover the Italian
possessions of the House of Austria, he was too
much alive to the immense difficulty of keeping
England out of the war if it should continue, not
to strain every nerve for the pacification of Europe.
First, he contrived gradually to secure from the
court an unwilling acquiescence in his endeavours,
before departing from our own neutrality, to bring
about a general peace. Nowhere was caution more
necessary. " Step by step," he said, " I can carry
the king and queen perhaps the road I wish, but if
I ever show them at a distance to what end that
road leads, they stop short." Second, he laboured
in the Cabinet, just as he was accustomed to do
in Parliament, by reasoning, persuasion, and steady
command of the facts as they were, to convert his
colleagues. For, says his brother in a casual
remark of much significance in the controversy

as to Walpole's arbitrary and dictatorial methods, "powerful as he was, he never would let his own opinion, in matters of State, prevail against the majority of them." [1]

The third and most exacting part of his task, besides holding back his own court and directing his own Cabinet, was to put such equal pressure now on the emperor, now on the cardinal, now on the court of Spain, as would force them to an adjustment. The emperor was bent on recovering his footing in Italy; the Queen of Spain, on securing Naples for Don Carlos, and his duchies for his brothers; France coveted aggrandisement on her eastern frontier at the expense of the Empire. The emperor was stubborn, proud, and dull. Fleury was naturally disposed to peace, but his hand was forced by colleagues with designs on Germany, and he was not without the duplicity of weakness. The Queen of Spain was a fury. The pensionary of the United Provinces was a martyr to the gout, was rough, peevish, and unmanageable; and the other Dutch leaders were all suspicious and distracted. Such were the personages with whom the British minister had to deal.

As usual, Walpole approached his difficulties step by step. The two maritime powers, Great Britain and Holland, held the key of the position. Any hope of assistance from them would harden the haughty and warlike temper of Vienna. On this side it was necessary to force into the mind of the emperor, that on no terms could he expect aid either from English or Dutch. On the other hand, the apprehension that the Dutch would act with vigour was the strongest of the reasons why France should come to honourable terms. If the maritime powers should hold aloof, she would suppose herself to have the Empire at her mercy. It will be seen how nice was the triple equipoise in which

[1] Coxe's *Mem. of Horace Walpole*, i. 328.

Walpole had to keep his representations at Vienna one day, at Versailles the next, and at the Hague every day.

After this exercise of delicate pressure on the emperor, a second leading object was to divide Spain from France. Each was in constant alarm lest the other should come to an accommodation with Vienna. Walpole caused France to be assured that if she did not make peace, a marriage would be agreed upon between an Austrian archduchess and one of the Spanish princes, to the detriment and isolation of the interests of France. Spain, on the other hand, was discreetly informed of the existence of secret communications between Versailles and Vienna. The scene is not particularly edifying to those who hope that politics are a branch of morals. Walpole's part, at any rate, was upright and consistent. He was no Machiavellian, engaged in a selfish match of fraud and craft, but an honest statesman, striving at once for the best interests both of his own country and of her neighbours. Instead of making England a party to a war in which she had not a shadow of concern, he made her the umpire and pacificator of Europe. In concert with Holland he submitted (1735) a plan of accommodation at the three courts. The plan contained no advantage to France, and so people laughed at it. Bolingbroke, however, shrewdly observed that Walpole was no fool, and there must be more in it than yet appeared. So it proved, for Walpole had discovered the design of France upon Lorraine, and that it might be possible for the emperor to find compensation in Tuscany. A new element of danger suddenly appeared in a quarrel between Spain and Portugal, but Walpole sent the British fleet to the Tagus as a hint of moderation to Portugal, and the mediation of England and France once more repressed an outbreak. After some months of further negotiation a general pacification was arranged. The Spanish Bourbon was installed in Naples and Sicily ; the Saxon elector was recognised as King of Poland ; Tuscany, on the death of the reigning grand duke, was to go to Francis of Lorraine, the destined husband of Maria Theresa ; Lorraine on this event (which happened very conveniently in 1737) was to belong to Stanislaus for life, and then to be ceded to France. A later generation saw the overthrow of this settlement—saw the Bourbons expelled from Naples and Sicily, the Austrians from Tuscany, and the French from Lorraine : we do not need to be told how much future trouble to the world was involved in the various arrangements of 1735–38. Walpole's defence for the cession of Lorraine—that it was a province of which France had taken and kept possession in every war in which she had been engaged—was unsatisfactory, but it may be counted a sufficiently good defence for the times. To modern sentiment there is something deeply repugnant in this insolent transfer of whole populations, with no more regard to race, to tradition, or to their own wishes, than if they were flocks and herds in a cattle-market. The idea of a federal and independent Italy was not altogether unknown. But to attempt to found a foreign policy on nationality in the first half of the eighteenth century, would have been generally deemed as impossible and as much of an anachronism, as in the second half of the nineteenth it would be to exclude or to ignore nationality. No effort on the part of Great Britain could have averted territorial rearrangement : it was something to effect it with the least possible confusion.

Walpole for once got perhaps even more credit than he deserved. Carteret declared that he always thought Walpole the luckiest dog that ever meddled with public affairs. Pulteney said it was a most

fortunate event for England, and whoever had
the honour of it, he was glad England had the
benefit of it. Bolingbroke put it that if the English
ministers had a hand in the peace, they had more
sense than he thought they had ; and if they had
no hand in it, then they had much better luck than
they deserved.

We now come to the most critical affair in Walpole's career. Having successfully steered through
foreign emergencies for so many years, in 1738
he encountered a storm in his own country, which
all his address and persistency were powerless to
quell, and which finally brought his power to destruction. The origins of the Spanish war of 1739
would furnish a long story. But the character
of that war is described in a single sentence. It
was, like the greater war of Pitt fifteen years later,
what Adam Smith calls a colony quarrel,[1] and its
object was to prevent the search of the colony ships
carrying on a contraband trade with the Spanish
main. By the Treaty of Utrecht a single British
ship was allowed to trade with Spanish America.
The annual ship became the colourable shelter of
an extensive illicit trade ; consorts followed her,
and she was incessantly replenished with fresh
supplies ; while at the same time, under thin
pretence of refitting and provisioning, other ships
carried on smuggling operations wherever they
could run a boat ashore. That all this was illegal,
that Spain was warranted in search and capture,
that occasionally these rights were harshly exercised
in distant seas and under proconsuls too far off to
be under control by the government at Madrid,
and that this harshness was often provoked by
the daring of the English traders, are all facts
which a few years after the war had broken out
nobody could be found seriously to deny. Burke
says that it was his fortune to converse with many

[1] *Wealth of Nations*, bk. iv. ch. 7.

of Walpole's enemies, who stirred up the clamour
against Spain as successfully as Burke himself in
after years stirred up the clamour against France.
" None of them," he says, " no, not one, did in the
least defend the measure, or attempt to justify
their conduct, which they as freely condemned
as they would have done in commenting on any
proceeding in history in which they were totally
unconcerned." [1]

For the moment no justification was necessary.
The merchants set the nation on fire with the tale
of atrocities on the Spanish main. Gentlemen
read letters to the House of Commons about seventy
of our brave sailors lying in chains in Spanish
dungeons. " Our countrymen in chains ! " cried
a city alderman in his place in Parliament, " and
slaves to Spaniards ! Is not this enough to fire
the coldest ? And shall we sit here debating about
words and forms while the sufferings of our countrymen call loudly for redress ? " Sea-captains came
to the bar of the House and told—not on oath, and
without liability to cross-examination—how free-
born Englishmen were loaded with irons, fed on
the vilest food, overrun with vermin, and driven
to work like galley-slaves for Spanish taskmasters.
The famous Captain Jenkins was produced to
inform Parliament how, seven years before, his
ship had been boarded by a Spanish *guarda-costa*,
and his ear had been brutally torn off, with the
taunt that he had better carry it to his king. On
being asked what he thought when he found himself in such ill plight, Jenkins replied, in a phrase
which became the cry of the hour, " I commended
my soul to my God and my cause to my country."
The neat balance of the sentence has not the ring
of the rough seafarer ; but the literary prompter,
whoever he may have been, knew his business.
When the country suffers itself to be swept by

[1] *Regicide Peace*, vol. viii. 147 (ed. 1818).

such stories as these, it ceases to be rigorous as to evidence and proof ; the possibility of exaggeration and invention made no difference in the effect. Recital of cruelty is the surest means of rousing the passionate indignation of Englishmen. They are not incapable of cruel deeds themselves, as some deplorable episodes in Ireland and the East and West Indies have shown. But to their honour it may be said that their sensibilities are readily touched ; and when, as in the present case, to humanity were added both national pride and commercial ambition, then, in the alderman's phrase, it was indeed idle to talk about forms and words, even though forms and words chanced to mean policy, legality, and international right.

Walpole agreed with the rest of the public that the conduct of the Spanish governors and captains deserved the sharpest resentment, but he believed that redress for the past and security for the future could be obtained by peaceable means. He knew that the fresh activity of the guardships in Spanish America was connected with Spanish objects in Europe, and he had satisfied himself that these objects could be more surely handled by diplomacy here than by buccaneers there. He insisted that war with the nation with whom our trade was greatest, would do us more harm than anything to be gained from it would do us good. He warned Parliament that France would certainly join Spain, and that, for various reasons, neither the emperor, nor Holland, nor Sweden would assist us. By these arguments he gained time, and a preliminary convention was made with Spain. Plenipotentiaries were to meet at Madrid to regulate the future relations of the two countries in respect of trade and navigation, and the various other questions in dispute. With unmeasured heat the Opposition denounced the convention, and re-echoed the passionate cry of the nation for war.

Walpole declared that war would be unjust, impolitic, and dishonourable. He carried the House of Commons with him by a slender majority of eight-and-twenty, but public opinion went every day farther away from peace. The pith of the English demand was abolition of the right of search, and right of search was what Spain would not concede, and after nine years of war still did not concede. Appeal to national pride proved to be a game at which two could play, and the insulting language of the Opposition roused in the people of Spain anger as hot against British buccaneers as that of Englishmen against Spanish guardships. The plenipotentiaries met in May (1739), but it was evident from the first that war was inevitable. The actual declaration was made in October, and was received in England with a frenzy of enthusiasm. "Ah! they are ringing the bells to-day," said Walpole; "they will soon be wringing their hands."

Then why did not Walpole resign? He had declared the war to be unjust, impolitic, and dishonourable; he had predicted disaster and confusion as its result; he was surrounded by colleagues who did not share his views, and who thwarted, embarrassed, and intrigued against him; neither court nor people went with him, and he was so conscious of the weakness of his position that he did actually and repeatedly press his resignation upon the king. Why did he not persist in it? That he was bound to refuse to have part or lot in a war which he believed, and had declared, to be unjust and dishonourable, it is wholly impossible to deny. This was not the case of the excise over again. There the public rejected a boon which he had gratuitously devised for them and proposed to them; the country would be no worse off after its rejection than it was before; the boon might be proffered again on another day. But to lend himself to an unjust and unnecessary war, was worse than if he had deliberately aided and abetted the South Sea scheme after denouncing it as fraught with national disaster.

The case against Walpole is too clear to deserve argument, but we are curious for explanation. It is not always safe to suppose the lowest motives to be the truest, even in politics. Those who find the key to Walpole's character in his thirst for power at any price and under all circumstances, have their explanation ready-made. It is not a very plausible one, on the face of it. If the retention of power had been his only thought, it would, as he said, have been his interest that there should be war ; [1] he would have been safer if he had flung himself, as Pitt, Pulteney, and the rest flung themselves, headlong into the current of public passion. But if Walpole was, on the other hand, a sound statesman, with clear vision and genuine public spirit, it is necessary to seek some other account of what was, on his own showing, not only connivance at a crime, but a gross miscalculation. As Bolingbroke said, Walpole was no fool. Considerations of real weight must have been present in his mind. We must remember, to begin with, that he had passed his whole life in surmounting difficulties, and bringing bad situations to good ends. He had not liked the Treaty of Hanover much better than he liked the Spanish war, yet he had turned it to good account. So with many other transactions in which he had been engaged. " I never heard," he said about this time, in a sentence which explains one great source of his strength, " *I never heard that it is a crime to hope for the best.*" He undoubtedly hoped that by remaining in office he would there be best able to seize the first opportunity, or if not the first, then the second or the third, of finding for

[1] Coxe, ch. li., iv. 55.

the war, mistaken as it was, a speedy and a safe issue. His adversaries were fully alive to this. One of their strongest charges against him was that he had no intention of making war in good earnest, and that he would cheat his own country by bringing the war to an end without forcing Spain to acknowledge the right of British vessels freely to navigate the American seas.

Then, again, Walpole must have known, as the event so swiftly proved, that his opponents, as they then stood, were incapable of forming a strong government, of conducting a war with vigour or making a peace with skill, and that not one of them was comparable to himself in experience, knowledge, or ability, either as negotiator or as administrator. Pitt as yet was only a declaimer, Carteret was a marvel of temerity and levity, and Pulteney, as we shall presently see, had neither nerve nor judgment for a crisis. Walpole might almost be excused for asking himself whether it could be his duty to leave the fate of his country to men who had shown themselves so recklessly unscrupulous and unprincipled, and who were destined, as he foresaw, to show themselves so profoundly incompetent. Finally, he may, without any baseness, have felt some of that special allegiance towards the king, which within limits we regard as a virtue when shown towards friends and colleagues in a party. The king's appeal, " Will you desert me in my greatest difficulties ? " was not one that after so many years of service Walpole could listen to with indifference. That he should have made himself an accomplice in an unjust and mischievous foreign war in order to help George II., was like Pitt's abandonment of the Catholic claim at the risk of a civil war to please King George's grandson. None of these pleas, however, stand good before the tribunal of history ; they may explain, but they cannot extenuate this notable error in Walpole's career, or efface the one stain on his political reputation.

The death of the emperor in 1740 was the signal for an immense outbreak of perfidy and rapine. Powers that had solemnly guaranteed the succession of his daughter to the hereditary dominions of her house, one after another poured troops into her provinces, and set about the dismemberment of Austria. Walpole urged a pacification between Maria Theresa and Frederick of Prussia, as the first step towards a union of Germany against the designs of France. But his counsels no longer commanded attention either at home or abroad, and in the astonishing changes wrought by Frederick on the European stage, he did not survive to play a part. When Walpole fell, as Ranke truly says, " it was not the fall of an ordinary minister, but the fall of the political system based upon the first union of the house of Hanover with the Regent of France. It was a return to the policy then abandoned of war against France and the Bourbon interest in Europe, and that at a moment when these once more had the upper hand both by land and sea." [1] He had brought the parliamentary constitution safely through its perils, though it was destined to new perils at a later epoch from the vigorous and obstinate reaction under George III. ; and the close of the constitutional movement at home left the way open for Pitt to conduct new enterprises abroad.

[1] Ranke's *History of England*, v. 405.

CHAPTER XI

THOSE who can recall the state of public feeling towards the coalition Government of Lord Aberdeen at the time of the Crimean War, will be able to realise the impatience and exasperation provoked by Walpole towards 1740. The general sentiment could not then organise and express itself with the extraordinary velocity and concentrated force—a velocity and a force not without peril of their own —to which we are so accustomed in the present day. But the great career which was opened by the genius and character of Pitt a few years later, demonstrated that even then it was possible for the tide of popular passion and enthusiasm to shake and to vanquish both court and Parliament. Walpole had placed himself in a completely false position, in which he could neither guide nor check, neither satisfy nor resist the judgment, prepossessions, passions, of the dominant orders and interests of the country. The national pride and temper were thoroughly roused. People had become profoundly fatigued with twenty years of good sense ; it seems as if nothing were so hard for a nation to sustain as a long course of mere prudence. That spirit which its admirers call enterprise, adventure, and energy, and which those who do not admire it, call cupidity in disguise, had become irresistible. It has been very truly remarked that the English bring to the government of their mercantile interests the same stiffness and pride as Louis XIV. brought to his dynastic interests. The war with Spain was a war for trade, for exclusive markets, for the mines of Peru and Potosi. It was a war for plunder. With such a mood in full blast, Walpole could not grapple. Burke put his finger upon the fatal spot when he said that Walpole, while professing to share the sentiments of his adversaries, opposed their practical inferences, and that this for a political commander is the choice of a weak post.[1] No observation could be more true, and the more popular the system of government, the truer is the application. To temporise, to manage, to find intermediate positions, to play a fine game, is in popular governments unintelligible and impracticable. The England of the Hanoverian kings was popular enough for this maxim to apply with all its force in moments of agitation, as Walpole found out.

The Duke of Newcastle saw his chance, and to Walpole's other embarrassments was now added personal dissension in the Cabinet. The duke flung himself eagerly into the designs of the war party. Lord Hardwicke, the Chancellor, always took sides with the duke. Wilmington, who had never forgotten his own miserable failure in 1727, thought that the opportunity of being first minister was again returning to him, as indeed it was. There were, in short, not more than three members of the Cabinet on whom Walpole could securely count. The king was frequently irritated at the minister's refusal to come in to his policy, but the staunchness of his character stood the test. "I do not care for the Opposition," he told Newcastle, "if all my servants act together; but if they thwart one another, then indeed it will be another case." The royal remonstrances could not abate the duke's peevishness and restlessness. Violent

---

[1] *First Letter on a Regicide Peace*, viii. 147.

altercations took place every day. " I oppose
nothing," said Walpole on one of these occasions,
" I give in to everything, am said to do everything,
am to answer for everything, and yet, God knows,
I dare not do what I think right. I am of opinion
for leaving more ships of Sir Challoner Ogle's
squadron behind, but I dare not, and I will not
make any alteration." The Archbishop pacifically
proposed postponement of the question, but Walpole refused. " Let them go," he cried, " let them
go." A struggle took place on a vacancy in the
Cabinet. In 1740 Walpole wished to make Lord
Hervey Privy Seal. The duke, to prevent the appointment, asked Carteret whether he would take
it. In the Cabinet he suggested that it should
be offered to Carteret. Walpole said he was not
sure that it would be accepted. The duke replied
that he would answer for that. " Oh," cried
Walpole, " I always suspected that you had
been dabbling there, and now I know it. But
if you make such bargains, I don't think myself
obliged to keep them." Hervey had the office,
and within a few months, when Walpole's hour
of danger came, Hervey turned his back upon
him.[1] In his memoirs he has described a scene
between the two ministers at the end of a long
meeting of the Cabinet, which deserves to be
transcribed :

Just as Sir Robert Walpole was upon his legs to go
away, the Duke of Newcastle said, "If you please, I would
speak one word to you before you go "; to which Sir
Robert Walpole replied, "I do not please, my lord ; but
if you will, you must."—" Sir, I shall not trouble you
long."—" Well, my lord, that's something ; but I had
rather not be troubled at all. Won't it keep cold till
to-morrow ? "—" Perhaps not, sir."—" Well, come then,
let's have it "; upon which they retired to a corner of
the room, where his Grace whispered very softly, and
Sir Robert answered nothing but aloud, and said nothing

---

[1] Horace Walpole to Mann, 7th January 1741, i. 112.

aloud but every now and then, "Pooh! Pshaw! O Lord! O Lord! pray be quiet. My God, can't you see it is over?"[1]

The leaders of the Opposition had in 1739 taken the unwise step of seceding from the House, as an expression of their disgust at the ruin that the minister was bringing on the country. The House of Commons is the worst place in the world for *coups de théâtre*. Their secession, like that of Fox and his friends, was a great mistake, and when they perceived the difficulties that were thickening round their redoubtable opponent, they hurried back. The Parliament had now approached its last session, and both sides had their attention fixed on the general election. It was with a view of bringing on the topics of their whole case against the minister, that the Opposition in the beginning of 1741 introduced in both Houses of Parliament their famous motion, that an humble address be presented to his Majesty that he would be graciously pleased to remove the Right Honourable Sir Robert Walpole, Knight of the most noble Order of the Garter, First Commissioner, Chancellor and Under-Treasurer of the Exchequer, and one of his Majesty's most honourable Privy Council, from his Majesty's presence and counsels for ever. The debate in the Commons (13th February 1741) began at one o'clock in the afternoon in a crowded House. The passages were thronged, and some members had even come down so early as six in the winter morning to secure their seats. Sandys opened the assault, and on the same day Carteret made the same motion in the House of Lords. Their topics were common. In foreign affairs the great article of charge was that the minister had abandoned our old and natural ally, the House of Austria, and raised up our inveterate enemy, the House of Bourbon. In domestic affairs he had

[1] *Memoirs*, iii. 370, 371.

fraudulently mismanaged the South Sea settlement, had failed to reduce the national debt, and had swollen the expenditure on Spithead expeditions and Hyde Park reviews, while his unconstitutional conduct had been seen in a standing army of un- necessary numbers, costly and useless squadrons, parliamentary corruption, the erection of new and useless offices, a swollen civil list, heavy taxation, and the dismissal of officers for voting against the excise scheme. These acts of profligate impolicy and maladministration were due to one who had arrogated to himself a place of French extraction, that of sole minister,[1] contrary to the nature and principles of the English constitution. Even, however, if no oversight, error, or crime were supposed in his public conduct, still in a free government " too long possession of power is dangerous." It was not necessary to prove him guilty of specific crimes ; as things stood, the mere dissatisfaction of the people and their suspicion of his conduct were sufficient causes for his removal from the counsels of the king.

The motion had no sooner been made than it was proposed that Walpole should withdraw, on the strength of a well-known practice of the House, that a member against whom an accusation has been brought should retire while his conduct is being inquired into. Both this, however, and the hardly less absurd amendment that he should be heard in his own defence and then withdraw, were dismissed. After a long and vehement discussion, in which Pulteney and Pitt were most conspicuous in the attack, Walpole wound up the debate in a speech which, so far as we can judge from the condensed report, was marked by an animation, comprehensiveness, and dignity worthy of a great

---

[1] Richelieu first assumed the quality of Prime Minister, and it was for long as odious in France as it became a century later in England. See *Œuvres du Card. de Retz*, i. 281 (ed. 1870).

minister defending a long and powerful government
of the affairs of a great nation.[1]

He vindicated his foreign policy and his financial
administration; taunted his enemies for reproach-
ing government with pusillanimity if they did not
interfere in foreign affairs, and with Quixotism if
they did; asked how he could answer charges
that were not specific, and were substantiated by
nothing more tangible than common fame and
public notoriety; insisted that if he had governed
by means of corrupt and profligate expenditure, then
King, Lords, and Commons for twenty years must
all have been his dupes or accomplices, which
was surely proving too much; declared that the
war had from the beginning been carried on with
as much vigour as was consistent with our safety
and our circumstances when the war broke out;
and, finally, came to an end with a warm denial of
charges of gratifying personal ambition, usurping
sole authority, grasping at emoluments or grants for
himself, or placing those connected with him in posts
of responsibility or trust for which they were unfit.

It is no esoteric secret confined to the precincts
of Parliament, that a taunt, or a personality, or
an appeal to any peculiar combination of parties,
often goes further for purposes of debate than
either lofty declamation or weighty reasoning.
Walpole opened his speech with what was the
most apt and vital part of it, a vigorous assault
upon the composition of the assailing body. The
Jacobites, he said, distress the government they
would fain subvert; the Tories contend for party
prevalence and power; the Patriots, impatient for
office, clamour for change of measures, but mean
only change of ministers. "A patriot, sir! why,
patriots spring up like mushrooms! I could raise
fifty of them within the four-and-twenty hours. I
have raised many of them in one night. It is but

---

[1] The minutes of the speech are given by Coxe, ch. lvi. vol. iv. p. 184.

refusing to gratify an unreasonable or an insolent demand, and up starts a patriot."

The coalition which Walpole denounced, did not hold together until the division. The movement had been ill concerted. It was devised by some of the malcontent Whigs, without consulting the Tories. Not even all the Prince of Wales's men voted. The most surprising event of the debate was the declaration of Shippen that he regarded the motion as only a scheme for turning out one minister and bringing in another; that it was quite indifferent to him who was in and who was out; and that he would give himself no concern in the question. When the time came, he and thirty-four of his friends walked out. Bolingbroke lost all patience with virtue so maladroit. The conduct of the Tories, he said, is silly, infamous, and void of any colour of excuse. It was certainly hard to reconcile with their general conduct on other occasions.

The motion was thrown out by 290 against 106 in the Commons, and 108 against 59 in the Lords. It was noticed that 500 members were present at the height of the debate, so that more than a hundred must have gone away without voting. The majority was crushing so far as it went, but the Opposition had been able to state their view of the issue before the constituencies and their owners. As a Jacobite well said, *it marked Walpole out to the nation.* The advantage of concentrating attention on a single personality, whether that attention be friendly or hostile, is a cardinal maxim among the mysteries of electioneering. That Walpole felt himself and his policy in deeper and more perilous waters than he had ever to face before, is certain. This was the time when his son drew that melancholy picture of him, almost the only melancholy one there is:

" He who was asleep as soon as his head touched the pillow, for I have frequently known him snore ere they

had drawn his curtains, now never sleeps above an hour
without waking ; and he, who at dinner always forgot
he was minister, and was more gay and thoughtless than
all his company, now sits without speaking, and with his
eyes fixed for an hour together."

It has even been contended, incredible as it
may seem, that Walpole himself, the most powerful defender of the Revolution, at this time made
overtures to the Pretender. It will be allowed
that very strong proof is needed to confirm a story
so opposed to all the rational probabilities of the
case ; but the mystery ought not to be passed over,
and Lord Stanhope is surely in the right when he
censures Coxe for omitting all mention of the
document from which the mystery arises, though
Coxe must have had it in his hands. The story
is this. Among Walpole's papers was found a
letter from James, dated from Rome in July 1739,
and endorsed in Walpole's own writing as being
an original letter, as having been addressed and
given in Rome to Carte, the Jacobite historian,
and as afterwards delivered to himself by Carte in
September. The letter is a reply from James to
some message transmitted to him by Carte from
an important person in England, to the effect that
this person wished well to James and his cause,
and had it in his power to serve both. The message
would seem to have asked for the old assurances
that the King, if restored to the throne, would
protect the Church of England and inflict no
vengeance on the Hanoverian princes. These assurances James was, of course, perfectly ready to
give, but he evidently distrusted the authenticity
of the message. " The message you bring," he
says to Carte, " could not but appear very singular
and extraordinary to me, because *you deliver it
only from second hand*, and that I have *no proof
of your being authorised by the person in question*,
who cannot but feel that it is natural for me to

mistrust what may come from him." [1] Carte, we must remember, though a strong and an honest Jacobite, was not a regular political agent by profession ; he was a student, and was at this time immersed in research for the purposes of his history of England. Part of that research he was at the moment industriously prosecuting in the royal archives in Paris, and no doubt he made frequent journeys between the two capitals. But James evidently felt it impossible to believe that a man of this stamp was likely to be chosen by Walpole as the bearer of so delicate and dangerous a communication.

If the letter had not borne Walpole's own endorsement, nobody would believe that it was he to whom James referred. Everybody would then have taken it for granted that it was an intercepted letter, and that the reference was to one of the malcontent Whigs in opposition. As it is, two important facts are to be observed. The author of the message, whoever he was, did not communicate his good wishes towards the Pretender direct to Carte, but to some third person. We are asked to assume, therefore, that Walpole, one of the wiliest of men, actually told somebody else to tell Carte that he wished well to the Pretender, and had his interest at heart. Next, Carte was unable to satisfy James that he had any authority to bring the message at all. In other words, these views, so absolutely irreconcilable with every act and utterance of his life, so profoundly important, so extremely dangerous, must have been thrown out by Walpole fortuitously, gratuitously, aimlessly, and without authority to anybody to convey them to the only man from whom he could expect any return for these momentous confidences. The only document that we have, therefore, cannot reasonably be taken as good evidence for so startling a state-

[1] Stanhope's *Hist. of England*, iii. Appendix, 50, 51.

ment as that Walpole made overtures to the Pretender, either insincerely, with a hope of winning
James's support at the general election (which was
more than two years off at the time of these overtures), or for any other purpose whatever.

Two hypotheses occur to us. The one is that
Walpole had nothing at all to do with the message ; that the sender of it was somebody else in his
camp ; and that Carte gave Walpole James's letter
to convince him that grave designs were afoot,
and that it was time for the minister to recognise
Jacobite power and influence. The other explanation is that in conversation with Carte's informant,
Walpole may have in general terms admitted the
possibility, in the event of a war and all the difficulties and complications of war, of a strong reaction
setting in against the House of Hanover ; he may
further have intimated the apprehension, which for
that matter had never for twenty years been absent
from his mind, and was the basis of his whole policy,
that if the Pretender would make declarations in
favour of the Church and against vindictive retalia-
tion, he might have a chance of restoration to the
throne of his ancestors. This was mere matter of
opinion on the facts. The Jacobite plotter was the
most credulous being in existence, and it is easy to
conceive that language of this kind, filtered through
several channels, may have emboldened Carte to give
James a message, in whose significance even the
Pretender himself, as his words show, did not for
a moment believe. This is the explanation of the
mysterious paper which seems to us to have fewest
difficulties. No explanation can have so many as
that which assumes that Walpole entered into a
dangerous intrigue for the bare chance of two or
three votes. This is the most incredible of all, not
merely because the intrigue would have been disgraceful, but because he must have known that it
would be futile.

The general election took place at midsummer (1741). The Duke of Argyll exerted all his influence against Walpole in Scotland, where the affair of Captain Porteous had not been forgiven. Then, as now, Scotland was almost unanimous, and only six out of the forty-five members were for the court. The twenty-one boroughs of Cornwall, under Lord Falmouth and other patrons, proved almost as unfavourable. The Cornish Tories had made a vigorous attack in the election of 1734, but had failed ignominiously. They succeeded in 1741, partly because the Falmouth influence had gone over to them, and partly because the Prince of Wales now actively intervened, and his power, as Duke of Cornwall, of asserting dormant or disputable rights, was too dangerous to be left out of account by these small corporations. When the time came, it was the Scottish vote and the Cornish vote that destroyed the minister. Walpole's attempt to divide the coalition between the malcontent Whigs, the Tories, and the Jacobites, which had been successful in the House, failed in the country; and the world beheld the curious sight of all the influence of the Pretender being thrown into the same scale with all the influence of the heir to the throne.

When the new Parliament met, Walpole's friends were sanguine enough to look for a majority of forty, and they calculated that a good majority, like a good sum of money, tends to make itself bigger. In our time we should know to a man, on the morrow of a general election, how the newly-chosen members would go, and whether they were for or against the government of the day. In the time of patrons and boroughmongers the caprice, the ambition, the selfishness of the individual had wider scope, and made calculation impossible. Not a day was lost before the two hosts eagerly joined battle. On the address Pulteney made a grand attack, to which

Walpole replied, as his party thought, with as much health, spirits, force, and command as ever. He showed that he meant to fight every inch. He flung aside the charge that he was answerable for all the public troubles. Was it he who had raised war in Germany, or advised war with Spain, or killed either the Emperor Charles or the King of Prussia, or been the adviser of Frederick or of the King of Poland, or kindled the war between Muscovy and Sweden ? He had brought about not one of these critical events ; but if they meant to turn him out, the sooner he knew it the better ; and if any man would move for a day to examine the state of the nation, he would second it. Chesterfield, he said, was right in telling the Lords that this was a time for truth, for plain truth, for English truth.

The unresting sea itself is less inconstant than are the moods of the House of Commons. After their chief's defiant speech, ministerialists had flocked home to their suppers in brilliant spirits ; but when the serious work of deciding election petitions began on the following afternoon, they were promptly awakened to the dangers in front. Disputed returns were then decided, not as now by a judicial tribunal, nor as in an interval between then and now by select committees, but by the whole House, and without a pretence of judicial impartiality. The petitions were settled by purely political considerations. The engagement opened with a division on one of the Cornish petitions. The minister won, but he won only by seven out of four hundred and thirty-seven. The alternative of Downing Street or the Tower was thus seen to be a startling possibility. The next trial of strength was the election of the chairman of committees. Excitement was raised to the keenest pitch, for there was an uncertain band whose votes would depend on their instinct for a majority, or who, if they could not trust their instinct, would abstain. In either

case the issue was doubtful. Two great party
dinners were held at two taverns, and after dining
at six o'clock, the House met in that tumult of hope,
fear, expectancy, confidence, indecision, that on
such high occasions quickens the pulse of the dullest
and the coolest. The lobbies were crowded, for
four hundred and eighty members out of a gross
total of five hundred and fifty-eight voted.

The tellers at last, amid breathless suspense,
announced the numbers. Walpole's nominee was
beaten by a majority of four. Pulteney and his men
raised a great shout, loud, fierce, and long,—the
exultant rebound after twenty years of unbroken
defeat. For twenty years they had been fortified
by the accession of one man of genius after another ;
for twenty years they had exhausted the resources
of wit, passion, and power in debate ; they had
practised every manœuvre in the art of parliamentary tactics ; they had divided only once in a
session, and they had harassed the foe with divisions ; they had taunted him with parsimony, and
reviled him for profusion ; they had held him up to
contempt for clinging to peace, and to execration
for running the risk of war ; they had scourged him
in public prints, and stealthily sapped him at court ;
and yet after twenty years of ingenious and relentless effort, only a few months before this night they
had been so baffled that they had actually marched
away in the sullenness of defeat and despair, leaving their adversary smiling, composed, unhurt, the
master of the field. And now at last the spell was
broken. They suddenly held their enemy at bay.
They had no right to the stern joy of victors in a
great public cause, but we cannot wonder that their
exultation was the most boisterous that had ever
been heard within the walls of Saint Stephen's
Chapel, or that some of the wilder among them even
reminded one another that *forty-one* was a date of
ill omen for tyrant ministers,—it was just a hundred

years since patriots had brought the guilty Strafford to the block.

The division lists began to fluctuate. For a few days after the first defeat, the minister had small majorities. Government won by seven, by twenty-four, by twenty-one, then they lost by four, by one,—so nice was the balance. On the important question of the Westminster petition, their men were thrown out by a majority again of four. There was no baseness to which men did not stoop. A young Irish peer was brought in for Winchelsea by the court. His competitor, though he had only a single vote at the election, presented a petition. The sitting member made a heroic speech, then went across to the Opposition, and promised if they would withdraw the Winchelsea petition, he would support them on the case of Westminster. This single vote lost Walpole one of the questions connected with that decisive event. Every point was fought, and the sittings were longer than ever were known. His opponents sank so low in their exasperation as to bethink themselves of Saturday sittings, as an ingenious means of depriving him of the air and exercise without which he could not live. Sir Robert held to his post, and made speeches at four o'clock in the morning as strong and as full of spirit as his speeches had ever been. His sons hoped that as soon as he had gained success enough for honour, and made the majority secure, he would be induced to quit the scene and end his career with some years of repose. But the veteran only laughed over the supper-table, and declared that he was younger than any of them.

The Christmas holidays arrived before the struggle was over, and were busily spent in urging the consciences and interests of wavering members. Spirit ran so high both indoors and outside, that not even the neediest member dared to offer his vote in return for a place, a pension, or cash down. There were over forty of them on whom neither side could count. Some of them gave first a vote for Opposition, then a vote for ministers, and the third time no vote at all; and then the order of their conscientious rotation began afresh. Horace Walpole had not long been back from Rome, where they had been electing a pope; the intrigues among members of Parliament reminded him of nothing so much as the dealings of the cardinals in the sacred conclave. Such was the desperate tenacity of the minister, that he actually wrung from the king permission to send an envoy informally to offer the Prince of Wales to raise his annual allowance from fifty to one hundred thousand pounds, to pay his debts, and to abandon all resentment and displeasure against him. The Prince replied, as Walpole might have been certain that he would reply, that he would listen to no such intimations, and that he desired to have no more of them until the retirement from power of the minister by whom he conceived himself to have been so deeply affronted and injured.

At the end of the recess, Pulteney instantly returned to the charge with a motion for a secret committee of twenty-one to inquire into the state of affairs, to send for persons and papers, and to give the king their advice. The thunder rattled from every oratorical battery. High speeches were made on both sides, including, besides Walpole and Pulteney, Pitt, Henry Fox, George Grenville, and Yonge. Yonge was the minister of whom Walpole said that nothing but such a character could keep down such parts, and nothing but such parts support such a character. When the debate was over, Pulteney, who, as has been said, always sat on the Treasury bench, cried in admiration to Sir Robert, "Well, nobody can do what you can." "Yes," replied Walpole, "Yonge did better." "No," Pulteney answered, "it was fine, but not of

that weight with what you said." The whip had
been vigorous. With the ardour that in a parliamentary crisis knows no bounds, they had dragged
men from sick-beds, and brought up lame, halt, and
blind. The minister's eldest son, as Auditor of the
Exchequer, had a residence that communicated with
the House of Commons. He was sheltering two or
three invalids there, until the question should be
put. The patriots stuffed up the keyhole with dirt
and sand, and the door could not be opened in time
for the division. When the division was taken the
members who voted made up 503, the greatest
number that had ever been in the House, and the
minister's majority in what would now be obviously
treated as a strict vote of confidence, fell to three.
It was evident that he was doomed.

Immediately after the overthrow of Pulteney's
proposal for a secret committee, the case of the
Chippenham petition was brought forward. On
the previous question the friends of the minister lost
by one, and on a later division on the merits by
sixteen. While the last division was being taken,
Walpole, who knew what was going to happen,
beckoned one of the members whose seat was
concerned, to come over and sit on the bench by his
side. " Young man," he said, " I will tell you the
history of all your friends as they come in, one
by one. Such an one, I saved his brother from
being hanged ; such another, from starving ; such
another, I advanced both his sons." It was not in
Walpole's nature to take reverses at a tragic pitch—
that fatal defect in political affairs. He was free
from all the cheap irony with which overstrained
idealists find consolation for their own misreadings
of human nature ; and the experience that " we
men are but a little breed," neither soured nor em-
bittered him. No statesman in history, not even
Cavour after the crash of Villafranca, ever faced
defeat more as a man should. This was the moment

when Lord Morton wrote to Forbes : " Last week
there passed a scene between Sir Robert and me by
ourselves, that affected me more than anything I
ever met with in my life.   He has been sore hurt by
flatterers, but has a great and an undaunted spirit,
and a tranquillity something more than human." [1]
Potter, the Archbishop of Canterbury, one night at
this time told Walpole that he had been lately
reading De Thou (an edition of De Thou had just
been published in England in seven stout folios),
and that he found a minister mentioned by him
who, having been long persecuted by his foes, at
last vanquished them, and the reason was *quia se
non deseruit.*   Walpole was as good as the man in
Thuanus.   His nerve never gave way, but, as he
informed the Duke of Devonshire, then in Ireland,
" the panic was so great among what I should call
my own friends, that they all declared my retiring
was become absolutely necessary, as the only means
to carry on the public business."

Between the two divisions on the Chippenham
petition, Walpole had made up his mind that
all must be over.   Subterranean communications
were carried on with some of the old Whig leaders,
and stipulations were made that Walpole should
be screened from all extreme proceedings.   The
younger Whigs, with Pitt at their head, strove to
make their own peace with the court by promising
more liberal securities for the minister than Pulteney
was ready to do.   They even undertook to answer
for the Prince of Wales.   Walpole always rated
these aspirants at what was then their true political
value, and declined the offer.   That the offer should
have been made, and on its rejection should have
been followed by unmeasured onslaughts on the
minister whom they had proposed to screen, is a
good test of the sincerity of all their heroic censures.

[1] *Culloden Papers*, 175, 11th February 1742. See also 5th January
1741–42.

When the arrangements with Pulteney were at last got into a fair train, Walpole sought an audience at St. James's. The king, who had so bravely supported him against the violence of foes and the perfidy of friends, was deeply moved; he fell on the minister's neck, wept, and kissed him, and begged to see him frequently.[1] Private intimation was sent to the Prince of Wales, and on the evening of February 2, 1742, when the final division against him took place, Walpole walked away for the last time out of that famous chamber, where for forty years he had laboured so assiduously for the national good, which had witnessed so many of his triumphs, which had been the scene of so long and undaunted a struggle against the most formidable enemies, and for which finally he had acquired new prerogatives and an immovable supremacy in the constitution of the kingdom.

The conflict began on the first of December in 1741. The House adjourned on the third of February, and on the ninth Walpole was created Earl of Orford. Besides this elevation it was arranged that he should receive a pension of four thousand pounds a year; the pension fell through until 1744, when Walpole was driven by his embarrassed circumstances to ask Pelham to obtain it for him—a reasonable favour which that plausible personage, who owed all to Walpole, granted with the worst possible grace. The minister's first wife had died in 1737. Then he married Mary Skerritt, with whom he had lived for several years, and who only enjoyed her new station for a few months. The child of this irregular union was now, as part of the royal recognition of her father's services, raised to the rank of an earl's daughter, and kissed hands, amid some gibes, as Lady Mary Walpole.

The drama did not end with Walpole's resignation. Scenes of almost unparalleled confusion

---

[1] Horace Walpole to Mann, 4th February.

rapidly ensued. The victorious coalition fell to pieces in the very hour of its triumph. Wyndham, who was justly described as the centre of union of the best men of all parties, had died on the eve of success (1740). They had no policy prepared, their tactics were not settled, and Pulteney, their leader, suddenly showed himself to be hopelessly bewildered and impotent. The country had taken the declamations of faction for the language of sincere belief and honest intention, and the popular expectations were boundless as they were distracted. There was a great cry for justice on the minister, and people were indignant at the criminal's audacity in daring to drive openly in the public streets. Others declared that they were not for blood, but that what the nation wanted was a good place bill, a pension bill, and triennial Parliaments. Some were for the reduction of the civil list, for life appointments, for abolishing regular troops. Others conceived the happily combined idea of doing away with all taxes, and carrying on the war with more vigour than ever. This wild babel of 1742 was the first example of the nemesis that awaits an Opposition that has been profligate in its promises. The bitterness of the disappointment was all in favour of the Jacobites, because it made people despair of any redress of their grievances from Parliament, and turned their minds towards a restoration. We are familiar with this particular effect of unreasonable expectations in France in our own day. This was always the Walpolean issue : a parliamentary commonwealth, or a legitimist restoration.

The one man who had a practical policy was the fallen minister, and his policy was the prosaic but very important one of keeping the Whig party together and continuing the government in Whig hands. That was what Burke meant by saying

that Walpole's whole theory of government was by
the instrument of party connection. That was,
and is, the secret of rule by Parliament. Walpole
had quitted Downing Street, but it was his influence
and address that still directed the contest. Pulteney, to whom all looked as the head of the new
government, on some scruple that he had once
declared that he would never take emolument or
office, accepted a seat in the Cabinet but declined
a department. No statesman has ever made such
an exhibition of infirmity as that of Pulteney in
1742. He told Lord Shelburne some years afterwards that there was no comprehending or describ-
ing the confusion that prevailed ; that he lost his
head, and was obliged to go out of town for three
or four days to keep his senses.[1] Yet it was not
courage in the ordinary meaning that failed him.
It was rather, as a contemporary observer said, a
sense of shame that made him hesitate at turning
courtier, after having acted patriot so long and
with so much applause. He was shackled, moreover, by the stipulations into which he had entered
before Walpole's retirement ; the feeling among
his followers and in the country was too strong
for him to let them be known, or to appear to
act on them ; and it may be that he had no alternative but to stand in the background until the
first fierceness of the storm had passed. When
that had gone, he found that his own chance
was ruined, and he was never able to retrieve it.
Though his action in this *gran rifiuto* was in-
expressibly weak, his judgment was clear. His view
was that the trunk of the government tree should
be Whig, but a few Tories might be grafted on it.
The Tories, he told the king, knew neither arithmetic nor foreign languages, and therefore could
not expect the first situations. The Tories themselves thought differently. They had quite enough

[1] *Life of Shelburne*, i. 47.

Q

arithmetic for quarter-day. They were all for a clean sweep, the obliteration of old parties, and government on a Broad Bottom, in which they should have their share. Bolingbroke hurried over from his meditations on the sweets of retirement and the blessings of exile, to share the day of glory with the men whose plans he had inspired. The clever plotter found that it was he who had been duped. The malcontent Whigs had no intention of dividing the spoil. The result of this discrepancy was in a few weeks a complete split between the two main sections of the old Opposition, the extinction of Pulteney in a peerage, and the maintenance of all Walpole's principal colleagues in office. Lord Wilmington was in name the head of the government, Newcastle, Hardwicke, Pelham, Yonge, all remained, and the only change of real importance was the admission of Carteret to be Secretary of State with the direction of foreign affairs.

The next question after the division of places was the punishment of the minister. There was much wild talk of impeachment, and articles were even prepared. But very little reflection showed that no crimes had yet been brought home to the impenitent criminal, and that there was nothing firmer to stand on than the hollow topics of parliamentary invective. Then they fell back upon a bill of pains and penalties, until they remembered that though such a bill might pass the House of Commons, it would certainly be thrown out by the Lords, and might not even receive the assent of the king. Walpole had no doubt done what he could to make certain of his own security from the old-fashioned vengeance on fallen ministers. All ended in the appointment of a secret committee of the House of Commons to examine into the last ten years of Walpole's administration. This body was finally composed of twenty-one members, only two of whom were friendly to the incriminated man. They set to work with all the zeal of party and personal hatred, summoned agents, and ransacked papers. The papers disclosed nothing. Scrope, secretary of the Treasury, who knew more Treasury secrets than anybody else, would tell them nothing. He said he was fourscore years old, and did not care whether the last few months he had to live were spent in the Tower or not ; the last thing he would do should be to betray the king, and next to him the Earl of Orford.

Walpole meanwhile only laughed at the secret committee. He laughed at a truly iniquitous bill which was brought in to aid the baffled committee, by giving an indemnity to anybody who would make discoveries as to the disposition of offices, or any payment or agreement in respect thereof, or concerning other matters belonging to the conduct of Robert Earl of Orford. The Lords threw out this odious project. Of the proceedings of the secret committee enough has been said on a previous page (111). As a grand exposure of the fallen minister, it was generally felt to have proved a complete failure. The mob had for a time daily carried his effigy in procession to the Tower. Horace Walpole one day ran up to one of these mobs to see what was the matter, and found a silly female figure, attended by three mock footmen, and labelled "Lady Mary." The popular fury and contempt soon died away. When Pulteney by a ruinous error of judgment allowed himself to be made Earl of Bath, public wrath found a new channel. Walpole's friends kept faith in a star which had been so long in the ascendant. His house was more crowded than it had ever been. One night in the summer (1742) his son took him to Ranelagh. "It was pretty full," says Horace, "and all its fulness flocked round us ; we walked with a train at our heels like two chairmen going to fight, but they were extremely civil and did not crowd him or say the least impertinence." When he went to the levee, his former master could not conceal his delight at seeing again the friend and author of so many good counsels, and the new ministers were in an agony lest the king should call him into the closet. They all, however, kept that fair countenance which often among political men hides such dismal emotions. They came and spoke to him, and he had a long and jovial talk with Chesterfield. Nobody seemed to bear anybody else malice. The Duke of Newcastle gave his colleagues a dinner one Sunday at Claremont; the servants got drunk and the coachman tumbled off the box on the way back. They were not far from Richmond, and the innkeeper told them that perhaps Lord Orford would lend them his coachman. So Walpole's coachman drove Pulteney, Carteret, and Limerick home. Carteret at a levee came up to thank him, the Duke of Newcastle standing by. "Oh, my lord," said Walpole, "whenever the duke is near overturning you, you have nothing to do but to send for me, and I'll save you."

Within a year of his fall the tide had begun to turn. The public had found out the imposture. They drank Sir Robert's health in all the clubs in the city, were for making him a duke, and straightway putting him back at the Treasury. They saw all in distraction : no union in the court; no certainty about the House of Commons; Lord Carteret making no friends, the king making enemies, Mr. Pelham in vain courting Pitt, Pulteney unresolved.[1] The common story that Walpole now retired to his plantations and his pictures in Norfolk, conveys a false impression. He was in fact only a degree less important and less closely attentive to every turn of affairs, both at home and abroad, than if he had still been in office.

---

[1] Horace Walpole to Mann, 12th October 1743, i. 275.

Pelham and others of his colleagues went to visit him, and constantly corresponded with him. Wilmington died in 1743, and after a struggle with Carteret, Pelham, acting at every step under the direct advice of Walpole, secured the first post in the government. His mentor from Houghton, adhering to his own cardinal maxim, warned him in characteristic language to confine his colleagues to one party,—" Whig it with all opponents that will parley, but 'ware Tory." Nor can we doubt that the other maxim present to Walpole was that the head of the government should have commanding influence in the House of Commons, and be a member of it. Pelham's administration lasted until his death in 1754. It narrowly escaped shipwreck almost before it left port. Carteret, thinking himself the ablest man in the Cabinet, tried to carry all with a high hand, treated the rest as ciphers, and trusted to his favour with the king to bring him through. Give any man the Crown on his side, Carteret used to say, and he can defy everything. Walpole's fall might have taught him how shallow was his maxim. He is never sober, says Horace Walpole, his rants are amazing; so are his parts and spirits. His colleagues fled to Walpole for shelter and counsel. By the beginning of 1744 the house in Arlington Street had again become the centre of affairs. Carteret and Pelham were his neighbours, and from their windows watched the bustle at his door. " I know you all go to Lord Orford," Carteret said, " he has more company than any of us—do you think I can't go too ? " As we shall see, he did go. The struggle between Carteret and the Pelhams was in one respect a counterpart of that which went on for the first twenty-three years of the reign of George III., and marked the strenuous effort of the king to break the dominion of the Whig families. In another aspect it was a question of the coherency

of Cabinets and the authority of the House of
Commons. Carteret ignored the Cabinet, where he
was outvoted by four to one, and he practically
renounced the Cabinet system. A wit said of him
that he would do better if he studied Parliament
more and Demosthenes less. These, and his rash
and unsound schemes in foreign policy, apart from
all old memories, were good grounds why Walpole
should never lend him the weight of his support.

Walpole throughout this difficult time behaved
like a man of honour and a faithful public servant.
" The king," says Horace Walpole, " is not less
obliged to Lord Orford for the defence of his crown,
now he is out of place, than when he was in the
administration. His zeal, his courage, his attention,
are indefatigable and inconceivable. He regards
his own life no more than when it was most his
duty to expose it, and fears for everything but
that." [1] When the king and Carteret were sorely
pressed by the thunders of Pitt and Chesterfield
against the Hanoverian troops, as well as by the
tricks and vacillations of the Pelhams, it was
Walpole who by the energy of his persuasion induced his friends to support the royal measures.
He had sat for two years in the House of Lords
without addressing them, but on an occasion
(February 1744) when he thought they were neglect-
ing certain information laid before them about the
Pretender, he suddenly rose and made one of his
finest and most animated speeches.[2] He had not
quailed before ministers when they were intriguing
and hunting him out of power, and he braved
unpopularity now, that they might use their power
for the public good. The same men were playing
the same game against Carteret, as Carteret and
they together had played against him. If any
one asks how Walpole's position had been more

---

[1] Horace Walpole to Mann, 16th February 1744, i. 290.
[2] Coxe, ch. lxii., iv. 333.

defensible towards his colleagues in the old Cabinet, than Carteret's was now, the answer is simple; Walpole had a majority in the House of Commons, and when he lost his majority, he gave up his post. Carteret never had a majority, he had not even a party. The Duke of Newcastle, said the king, is grown as jealous of Lord Granville (Carteret's new title) as he was of Lord Orford, and wants to be first minister himself. Pelham was jealous both of Granville and of his own brother, the duke. At last the struggle in the Cabinet grew too fierce to be prolonged, and the Pelham faction informed the king, just as Godolphin and Marlborough had informed Queen Anne in the case of Harley in 1708, that he must make his choice. The king in his distress sent for Walpole, who was then at Houghton, suffering miseries from stone. This move was almost certainly suggested by Lord Granville, — strange illustration of the irony of politics, for he was the man who had made the motion only three years before, that Walpole should be removed from the king's counsels for ever. Walpole discouraged reliance on Granville, as he had systematically done in the days of Queen Caroline, and sent messages to urge the king to abide by the wishes of the majority in the Cabinet. After an excruciating journey he found himself at Arlington Street. All the politicians flocked to his house, and thought he must speedily be minister again.

The political battle was settled, as Walpole would have it settled, against Granville. The Pelham interest, aided by the influence of Walpole, was preponderant in the House of Commons, and this was now the decisive consideration. The boroughmongers had forced the king to give up Walpole, and now they forced him to give up Granville. They patched up a coalition with the patriots, humoured Pitt and eventually overcame the king's reluctance to admit him to office, and formed that Broad-Bottomed administration from which every national blessing was fondly expected. Before many months had elapsed an insurrection broke out in the royal closet. The ministers tried to coerce the king by bringing seals, staves, keys, and commissions, and resigning in a body. Granville and Bath attempted to form an administration (March 1746). It lasted, as the wits said, forty-eight hours, seven minutes, and eleven seconds. All went swimmingly, until they found they had forgotten one little point, and that was to secure a majority in either House of Parliament. The old band returned in triumph. Granville laughed and drank, owned it was mad, but would do it again to-morrow. He was even daring and senseless enough to advise the king to go down to Westminster, and remonstrate from the throne with Lords and Commons assembled, against the usage that he had received. These were the men who had led the opposition to the great administration of Walpole.

To him the drama, in which he had long played a part so staunch, so manly, and so serviceable to his country and to Europe, was no longer an object of concern. He subjected himself to extraordinary and terrible treatment for his cruel malady, bore its torments with fortitude, retained his clearness of judgment to the end, and at length with little pain expired on March 18, 1745. His remains were conveyed from Arlington Street to Houghton, where they rest, like those of Edmund Burke at Beaconsfield, without commemorative monument or name.

THE END

Printed by R. & R. CLARK, LIMITED, *Edinburgh.*

34539759R00138

Made in the USA
Lexington, KY
09 August 2014